はしがき

本書はTOEIC® L&Rテスト受験を目指す初級から600点以上のスコア取得を目指す学生のためのテキストです。本書は全15Unitで構成されて〔　　　　　　　　　〕たことがない初心者でも順にステップを追うことにより確実にレベ〔　　　　　　　　　〕最初の3つのUnitではPart 1～Part 7各セクションの問題のタイ〔  〕EIC® L&Rというテストそのものに慣れ、先に進むために必要な〔　　　　　　　　〕に作られています。この3つのUnitの学習を通じて、自分の実力を〔　　〕目標点を設定し、その目標点に達するためには各Partでどのような対策を立てればよいか、その糸口が見えてくることでしょう。Unit 4以降は、頻繁に出題されるシチュエーション別に、全タイプの問題が含まれており、授業で実践的なTOEIC® L&R対策ができるようになっています。毎回時間を意識しながら各Partの問題を解くことにより、自分にとってどのPartが解答しやすいか、どのPartにどれだけ時間がかかるのかが実感できるようになり、TOEIC® L&Rテストに対する自信が少しずつ積みあがることでしょう。

本書を利用してしっかりとスコアアップを実現させるために特に以下の3つのことを実践していくことをこころがけてください。

1. TOEIC® L&Rテスト頻出ボキャブラリーを習得する

TOEIC® L&Rでは毎回繰り返し出題される語彙表現があります。各Unitに出てきた自分が知らなかった語彙表現は書き留めて、問題文の文脈の中で覚えていくようにしましょう。少しずつためていくだけでも大きな力となります。

2. 時間を意識して解答する

リーディングセクションを解くときには、常に時間を意識することが重要です。例えばPart 5の短文空埋め問題30問を7～12分で終えるようにすると、Part 7の読解問題でより多くの時間を使うことができます。今までゆっくりと英文を読んで解答することに慣れている人は、スピードが最も重要な要素の一つであることを意識するようにしましょう。Part 7の読解問題を解くときも必ず時間を意識するようにします。すべてを読まなくても、できるだけ早く設問と選択肢に目を通すことにより、必要な情報が載っている箇所だけを見つけるようにします。うまく時間が使えるようになることで必ずスコアがアップします。

3. リスニングの復習を徹底的にやる

今まであまり英語を聞いたことがないのでという人にとっては、テストの半分を占め100問もあるリスニングセクションは大きな難関です。授業で何度かリスニング問題を聞くだけでは十分な学習効果は得られません。授業で理解したリスニング問題の解き方や内容をしっかり理解したうえで、何度も繰

り返し聞くようにしましょう。さらにはその聞きなれた問題を利用して口に出すこと、例えばリピーティング（スクリプトを見て音を聞きながら同じように繰り返す）やシャドウイング（スクリプトを見ないで聞こえた音に自分の声をかぶせて言ってみる）を必ず習慣づけるようにするとリスニング力アップにつながります。

　やるべきことを習慣的に実践していけば、必ずTOEIC® L&Rテストのスコアはアップします。本書を利用していただいた学習者が一人でも多く目標点を達成されることを著者一同心から願っております。

　　　　　　　　　　　　　　　　　　　　　　　　　　　　　　　　　　川端　淳司

TOEIC® L&Rについて

TOEIC® L&R（TOEIC Listening & Reading Test）は、リスニングセクション100問、リーディングセクション100問の合計約2時間で200問に答えるマークシート式のテストです。解答はすべて問題用紙とは別の解答用紙に記入していきます。テストは英文のみで構成されており、試験中メモをとることはできません。問題冊子は試験終了時に解答用紙とともに回収されます。

各パートの問題数

リスニングセクション（約45分）			リーディングセクション（75分）			
Part 1	写真描写問題	6問	Part 5	短文穴埋め問題		30問
Part 2	応答問題	25問	Part 6	長文穴埋め問題		16問 (4×4)
Part 3	会話問題	39問 (3×13)	Part 7	読解問題	1つの文書	29問
	会話 + 図版 (graphics)				複数の文書	25問 (5×5)
Part 4	説明文問題	30問 (3×10)				
	説明文 + 図版 (graphics)					

テストの結果は合否を判定するものではありません。10～990点の「スコア」として獲得した点数が表示され、試験の結果は受験後約1ヶ月で郵送されます。

このテストはまた、現在の英語力がどの程度であるか客観的に確認できるだけでなく、就職活動や入学試験に、卒業後社会人になってもキャリアアップのために活用できるものとして広く普及しています。

参考／一般財団法人 国際ビジネスコミュニケーション協会
https://www.iibc-global.org/toeic.html ▶

CONTENTS

リスニング Part 1 & 2
リーディング Part 5 & 6

Part 1 リスニング「写真描写問題」攻略

　TOEIC® L&RのPart 1では1枚の写真について4つの短い説明文を聞きます。4つのうち写真を最も適切に描写しているものを選ぶ問題です。実際のテストでは6問出題されます。

　写真のタイプとしては、一人の人物が掲載されているもの、複数の人物が掲載されているもの、さらに人以外の動物や物が掲載されているものがあります。

■　実際の問題を解いてみる前に、まずは次の写真を見て、できる限り多くの英文を思い浮かべてみましょう。

例 題

1.

2.

■　次に、写真を描写する英文を聞いて、次の空所を埋めましょう。　🔊 Audio① 02-03

1. The bird is _____ on a _____ of the _____ .

2. The man is _____ a _____ mountain.

Part 1 リスニング「写真描写問題」実践　🔊 Audio① 04-06

■　次の写真について、4つの説明文の中から最も適切なものを1つずつ選びましょう。

1. Ⓐ Ⓑ Ⓒ Ⓓ

2. Ⓐ Ⓑ Ⓒ Ⓓ

1. (A) The woman is wearing a _____ and _____.
   (B) The woman is holding a _____.
   (C) The woman is rolling up her _____.
   (D) The woman is using a _____.

2. (A) _____ is gushing into the air.
   (B) The _____ is overflowing its banks.
   (C) A few _____ are flying in the sky.
   (D) _____ are trying to catch fish.

Part 2 ▶ リスニング「応答問題」攻略

　TOEIC® L&RのPart 2では1つの質問または発言と、3つの応答を聞きます。3つの応答から質問または発言に対して最も適切なものを選ぶ問題です。実際のテストでは25問出題されます。

　はじめに1つ英文を聞きますが、ここでは質問になる英文の場合と、質問になっていない発言となる英文を聞く場合があります。質問になる英文の場合は、どのような疑問詞を使った質問文であるかを聞き分けられるかがポイントになります。

■ 実際の問題を解いてみる前に、まずは次の英文から考えられる応答文を自分で考えてみましょう。

例 題

1. How long has it been since you graduated from high school?

   _____

2. Do you mind if I invite my friend Bob over?

   _____

■ 次の質問について、3つの応答文の中から最も適切なものを選びましょう。　🔊 Audio① 07-09

1. How long has it been since you graduated from high school?　Ⓐ　Ⓑ　Ⓒ
2. Do you mind if I invite my friend Bob over?　Ⓐ　Ⓑ　Ⓒ

Part 2 ▶ リスニング「応答問題」実践　🔊 Audio① 10-13

音声を聞いて応答として最も適切なものを1つずつ選びましょう。

1. Mark your answer.　Ⓐ　Ⓑ　Ⓒ
2. Mark your answer.　Ⓐ　Ⓑ　Ⓒ
3. Mark your answer.　Ⓐ　Ⓑ　Ⓒ

TOEIC® L&RのPart 5では4つの選択肢の中から最も適切なものを選び、不完全な英文を完成させる問題が問われます。実際のテストでは30問出題されます。

英文の内容は様々ですが、空所で問われる文法事項にはある程度のパターンと特徴があります。

まずは問題を解く前に、4つの選択肢をよく見てどのような事柄が問題として問われているか考えてみましょう。問われている事柄が分かれば短い時間で正答を見つけることができるはずです。

■ 次の英文を完成させるのに最も適切なものをそれぞれ1つずつ選びましょう。

1. The first ingredient of a nation's economic system is ------- natural resources.

   (A) it

   (B) them

   (C) its

   (D) their

2. Organized labor continues to be an important political and ------- force today.

   (A) economically

   (B) economy

   (C) economical

   (D) economic

3. Concern over gun violence has been building even as the number of Americans killed by guns -------.

   (A) fall

   (B) has fallen

   (C) has been fallen

   (D) have fallen

次の英文を完成させるのに最も適切なものをそれぞれ1つずつ選びましょう。

1. The U.S. Food and Drug Administration has ------- Gyrotech's colon cancer drug Ahoy.

   (A) approval

   (B) approves

   (C) approved

   (D) approving

2. Wall Street gets its name from a wall ------- across Lower Manhattan in 1653.

   (A) to build

   (B) building

   (C) built

   (D) was built

3. Prices normally ------- around a point which will give a return approximately equal to the prevailing rate of interest.

   (A) fluctuate

   (B) fluctuation

   (C) fluctuating

   (D) was fluctuated

4. On average, the standard of living today has ------- fairly steadily from that several centuries ago.

   (A) risen

   (B) raised

   (C) arisen

   (D) aroused

5. Airlines and hotels are coming up with new ways ------- travel easier for customers.

   (A) making

   (B) made

   (C) make

   (D) to make

TOEIC® L&RのPart 6は、空所に入る最も適切な語または一文を4つの選択肢の中から選び、不完全な文書を完成させる問題で、実際のテストでは4題16問出題されます。

Part 5の「短文穴埋め問題」と同様に、英文の内容は様々ですが、空所で問われる事柄にはある程度のパターンと特徴があります。また英文一つにつき1問だけ文を補う問題が出題されています。

Part 5と同様、4つの選択肢をよく見て、どのような事柄が問題として問われているか考えてから問題を解きましょう。

例 題

次の文書を完成させるのに最も適切なものをそれぞれ1つずつ選びましょう。

Questions 1-3 refer to the following letter.

Kathy J. Tusher
4860 South Granada Street
Englewood, Colorado 83045
(303) 771-8108
July 14, 2020

Mr. Wallen P. Watson
Regional Sales Manager
Richard Pharmaceuticals
2100 E. Marketplace Road
Denver, Colorado 80454

Dear Mr. Watson:

Are you searching for a salesperson in the Denver area who is outgoing, confident, and loyal to a company and product she believes in? If so, then I am the person you are looking for. I am presently ---**1.**--- (five years as retail sales manager for a home oxygen and medical equipment company) but now plan to take the next step in my sales career.

My background as a registered nurse fits well with pharmaceuticals. ---**2.**---. I want to meet you to learn more about Richard Pharmaceuticals. Please contact me at ---**3.**--- earliest convenience.

Enthusiastically,
Kathy J. Tusher

1. (A) employment
   (B) employees
   (C) employed
   (D) employing

2. (A) Because of my nursing background, I will be able to explain your products with professional expertise.
   (B) I have taught at a primary school, so I can teach many subjects to your customers.
   (C) Since I used to work at a school, I'm very patient.
   (D) Considering my background, I will be able to explain how to be a good nurse.

3. (A) it
   (B) your
   (C) him
   (D) theirs

Part 6 リーディング「長文穴埋め問題」実践

次の文書を完成させるのに最も適切なものをそれぞれ1つずつ選びましょう。

Questions 1-3 refer to the following article.

Napa Valley, a little over 35 miles in length, is home to over 150 wineries, most of which line Highway 29. Many of the large wineries such as the Robert Motaro Winery in Oakville and Angelhead Napa Valley in Rutherford offer guided tours of ---**1.**--- facilities including the underground limestone caves and storage casks. And yes, for a small charge, you can taste the wines. ---**2.**---. Most visitors will find wine tasting is both ---**3.**--- and educational.

1. (A) it   (C) itself
   (B) you   (D) their

2. (A) Most of the wineries were built a couple of centuries ago.
   (B) There are many fascinating varieties to sample.
   (C) You can enjoy making some on your own for free.
   (D) You will see many people eating there.

3. (A) enjoyable
   (B) enjoy
   (C) to enjoy
   (D) enjoyments

リスニング Part 3
リーディング Part 7 シングル・ダブルパッセージ

Part 3 リスニング「会話問題」攻略

　TOEIC® L&RのPart 3では短い会話を聞き、その後に続く設問に答えます。4つの選択肢から設問に対して最も適切なものを選ぶ問題です。実際のテストでは39問出題されます。

　Part 1とPart 2とは異なり、設問と選択肢が問題用紙に印刷されていますから、音声を聞く前に目を通して、設問のポイントを絞り込んでおくことが正解へのカギとなります。設問は全て疑問詞で始まります。一部の問題ではイラストや図が組み込まれています。

■ 実際の問題を解いてみる前に、まずは例題の設問から問われている内容を（　）内に書いてみましょう。

例題

1. What are the speakers discussing? （　　　　　　　　　　）

2. What position does the man most likely hold? （　　　　　　　　　　）

3. What will happen next? （　　　　　　　　）

■ 次に、選択肢に目を通し、必要な場合には（　）内にメモをしてみましょう。

1. **What are the speakers discussing?** 話者たちは何について話していますか。

   (A) The access code for Zeno （　　　　　　　）

   (B) A fire at a competing company （　　　　　　　）

   (C) A trip to a packaging plant （　　　　　　）

   (D) Protection for their computer system （　　　　　　　）

2. **What position does the man most likely hold?** 男性がついている地位として最も可能性が高いものはどれですか。

   (A) Salesman at Tripco （　　　　　　）

   (B) Telephone operator （　　　　　　）

   (C) The woman's subordinate（　　　　　　　）

   (D) The main hacker at Zeno （　　　　　　）

3. **What will happen next?** 次に何が起きるでしょうか。

   (A) The man will do some research. （　　　　　　　　）

   (B) The woman will call Tripco. （　　　　　　　）

   (C) The man will leave the company. （　　　　　　　　）

   (D) The woman will hack Zeno. （　　　　　　　）

1. **What are the speakers discussing?**

   (A) The access code for Zeno

   (B) A fire at a competing company

   (C) A trip to a packaging plant

   (D) Protection for their computer system

2. **What position does the man most likely hold?**

   (A) Salesman at Tripco

   (B) Telephone operator

   (C) The woman's subordinate

   (D) The main hacker at Zeno

3. **What will happen next?**

   (A) The man will do some research.

   (B) The woman will call Tripco.

   (C) The man will leave the company.

   (D) The woman will hack Zeno.

■ スクリプトの空所を埋めながら、音声の内容を確認しましょう。

🔊 Audio① 15

Questions 1 through 3 refer to the following conversation.

W: We need to [1]_____ _____ _____.

M: I agree. Hackers have already accessed the mainframe at Zeno.

W: Yes, and if they can get to our main competitor, we need to be [2]_____ _____ _____.

M: I think Tripco offers the best overall system protection. [3]_____ _____ _____ _____ _____ _____ ?

W: No, not yet. Please look into competing packages first. We need to consider various price options.

M: All right, I'll [4]_____ _____ _____ _____ _____.

■ まずは設問と選択肢の内容を20秒くらいで確認しましょう。その後、音声を聞いて設問に答えましょう。

1. **Where does the man most likely work?**

   (A) At an electrical power plant

   (B) At a car dealership

   (C) At a department store

   (D) At a battery factory

2. **Why is the woman calling?**

   (A) To buy a newer model

   (B) To check on the availability of parts

   (C) To confirm her service appointment

   (D) To speed up her delivery

3. **What does the man offer to do?**

   (A) Help the woman find a faster model

   (B) Reduce the service price

   (C) Connect the woman to another section

   (D) Serve as a mechanic

■ スクリプトの空所を埋めながら、音声の内容を確認しましょう。　↰ 🔊 Audio① 20

Questions 1 through 3 refer to the following conversation.

M: Hello, this is the [1]_____ _____, James speaking.

W: Hello, this is Mary Stewart, and I'm calling to ask if you have a [2]_____ for the Speedster in stock.

M: What year is your model?

W: It's a 2002.

M: Hold on a sec, let me check to see if we have one in stock.

W: All right. And while you're at it, could you also see if you have a generator? The whole electrical system needs attention, I think.

M: You're in luck. I see we still have both, though yours is an older model. Would you like me to [3]_____ _____ _____ _____ _____ _____ _____ to set up an appointment?

W: Yes, please. I was going to try to install them myself, but [4]_____ _____ _____, it's better to have your mechanics see to it.

TOEIC® L&RのPart 7では1つもしくは複数の文書に関する問題が出題されます。複数の文書については、2つの文書を読む場合と3つの文書を読む場合があります。実際のテストでは1つの文書に関する問題が29問、複数の文書に関する問題が25問出題されます。

使われている素材はレター、Eメール、メモ、広告、チャットやインスタントメッセージなどがあります。

文書の全てを読んでから設問に答えるのではなく、まずは英文のタイトルや冒頭部分に目を通し、主旨を素早く捉えることが重要です。おおよその主旨がわかれば、設問と選択肢に注目し、その中に含まれるキーワードを基に本文中の該当箇所を検索するようにすることで、素早く解答を選ぶことが可能です。

シングルパッセージ

■ 実際の問題を解いてみる前に、まずは設問文を読んで、問われている内容を（　）内に書いてみましょう。

1. What is this company selling?（　　　　　　　　　）

2. Which of the following statements is NOT true?（　　　　　　　　　）

■ 次に、選択肢に目を通して、必要な場合には（　）内にメモをしてみましょう。

1. What is this company selling?　　この会社は何を販売していますか。

   (A) Travel tours of beachfront land（　　　　　　　　　）

   (B) Newly listed stocks（　　　　　　　）

   (C) Lakeside cottages（　　　　　　　）

   (D) Coastal property（　　　　　　　）

2. Which of the following statements is NOT true?　　次のうち正しく述べられて**いない**ものはどれですか。

   (A) There are not many units available.（　　　　　　　　　）

   (B) The company thinks that there is no better time to buy than now.
       （　　　　　　　　　）

   (C) This offer will last indefinitely.（　　　　　　　　　）

   (D) A beautiful sunset can be enjoyed at the beach.（　　　　　　　　　）

■ それでは、実際に英文を読んで設問に答えましょう。

Questions 1-2 refer to the following notice.

PUBLIC NOTICE
NORTH CAROLINA OCEANFRONT
Liquidation Sale

Announced by Land Company

<u>FOR A LIMITED TIME ONLY</u>

According to a company spokesperson, "THIS IS THE TIME TO BUY"

— <u>Oceanfront like this is a once-in-a-lifetime opportunity</u>.

Properties included in the sale offer white sand and beaches, crystal clear waters, beautiful sunsets, beachfront cabanas, and range from $40,000 to $100,000. Only a few will be made available at these prices.

---

1. What is this company selling?

(A) Travel tours of beachfront land

(B) Newly listed stocks

(C) Lakeside cottages

(D) Coastal property

2. Which of the following statement is NOT true?

(A) There are not many units available.

(B) The company thinks that there is no better time to buy than now.

(C) This offer will last indefinitely.

(D) A beautiful sunset can be enjoyed at the beach.

ダブルパッセージ

シングルパッセージの場合と同様に、まずは設問文だけを読んで問われている内容を確認し、2つのパッセージの内のどちらを読む必要があるか、考えてみましょう。

		パッセージ（○で囲む）
1.	Where does Maxwell Page work?	（ 1 / 2 ）
2.	Which is NOT mentioned in the job description?	（ 1 / 2 ）
3.	By what date should applicants respond to Maxwell Page?	（ 1 / 2 ）
4.	Why does Robert Nakata mention his classwork at Indiana State University?	（ 1 / 2 ）
5.	What did Robert Nakata send with his e-mail?	（ 1 / 2 ）

14 Unit 2 リスニング Part 3／リーディング Part 7（シングル・ダブルパッセージ）

《Passage 1》

Assistant Drafting Engineer wanted to draw up blueprints to engineering specifications for a medium-sized manufacturer of industrial component parts. Starting salary approx. $40,000 per year, depending on qualifications. University degree in mechanical engineering preferred, but candidates with related experience will be considered. Send resume to Maxwell Page, Rorty Manufacturers, Inc., 338 Henderson Park Drive, Muncie, Indiana 47389 or mpage@rortyman.com no later than September 30.

《Passage 2》

From: Robert Nakata
To: Maxwell Page
CC:
Subject: Assistant Drafting Engineer Position
Sent: Monday, September 21 10:02 A.M.

Dear Mr. Page:

I am writing in response to your advertisement for an assistant drafting engineer which appeared in the Help Wanted section of the September 20 edition of the Muncie Times. I believe that I am well qualified for this position. As you can see from my attached resume, I graduated from Indiana State University this past May with a B.S. in mechanical engineering. Although I do not have any experience working as a drafting engineer, I did study blueprint drafting and I am enthusiastic and hardworking. I am currently working part-time in Chicago but could easily return to Muncie on any weekday for an interview.

Please feel free to contact me if you need additional information or a letter of reference. I believe that I still have some of the blueprints which I submitted as classwork, too.

Sincerely,
Robert Nakata
rnakata@email.net

Questions 1-5 refer to the following advertisement and e-mail.

Assistant Drafting Engineer wanted to draw up blueprints to engineering specifications for a medium-sized manufacturer of industrial component parts. Starting salary approx. $40,000 per year, depending on qualifications. University degree in mechanical engineering preferred, but candidates with related experience will be considered. Send resume to Maxwell Page, Rorty Manufacturers, Inc., 338 Henderson Park Drive, Muncie, Indiana 47389 or mpage@ rortyman.com no later than September 30.

From:	Robert Nakata
To:	Maxwell Page
CC:	
Subject:	Assistant Drafting Engineer Position
Sent:	Monday, September 21 10:02 A.M.

Dear Mr. Page:

I am writing in response to your advertisement for an assistant drafting engineer which appeared in the Help Wanted section of the September 20 edition of the Muncie Times. I believe that I am well qualified for this position. As you can see from my attached resume, I graduated from Indiana State University this past May with a B.S. in mechanical engineering. Although I do not have any experience working as a drafting engineer, I did study blueprint drafting and I am enthusiastic and hardworking. I am currently working part-time in Chicago but could easily return to Muncie on any weekday for an interview.

Please feel free to contact me if you need additional information or a letter of reference. I believe that I still have some of the blueprints which I submitted as classwork, too.

Sincerely,
Robert Nakata
rnakata@email.net

1. **Where does Maxwell Page work?**

   (A) At a university

   (B) At a printing shop

   (C) At a manufacturing corporation

   (D) At a research center

2. **Which is NOT mentioned in the job description?**

   (A) Job duties

   (B) Job title

   (C) Salary

   (D) Benefits

3. **By what date should applicants respond to Maxwell Page?**

   (A) September 20

   (B) September 21

   (C) September 30

   (D) October 1

4. **Why does Robert Nakata mention his classwork at Indiana State University?**

   (A) He may have evidence of previous job-related experience.

   (B) He believes that his university is excellent.

   (C) He believes his studies may be related to this position.

   (D) He may have evidence of previous work experience.

5. **What did Robert Nakata send with his e-mail?**

   (A) His transcript

   (B) His resume

   (C) Some blueprints

   (D) Letters of reference

リスニング Part 4
リーディング Part 7 トリプルパッセージ

Part 4 リスニング「説明文問題」攻略

　TOEIC® L&RのPart 4ではアナウンスや電話のメッセージなどの説明文を聞き、その後に続く設問に答えます。4つの選択肢から設問に対して最も適切なものを選ぶ問題です。実際のテストでは30問出題されます。

　Part 3と同様に、設問と選択肢が問題用紙に印刷されていますから、音声を聞く前に目を通して、設問のポイントを絞り込んでおくことが正解へのカギとなります。一部の問題ではイラストや図が組み込まれています。

■ 実際の問題を解いてみる前に、まずは例題の設問から問われている内容を（　）内に書いてみましょう。

例 題

1. Where will guests stay? （　　　　　　　　　　　　　　　）

2. Who are the most likely listeners? （　　　　　　　　　　　　　）

3. What are guests expected to do? （　　　　　　　　　　　　　）

■ 次に、選択肢に目を通し、必要な場合には（　）内にメモをしてみましょう。

1. **Where will guests stay?** 　ゲストたちはどこに滞在するでしょうか。

　　(A) In animal sanctuaries （　　　　　　　　　　　）

　　(B) On tour buses （　　　　　　　　　）

　　(C) On houseboats （　　　　　　　　）

　　(D) In tents （　　　　　　　）

2. **Who are the most likely listeners?** 　聞き手として最も可能性が高いのは誰ですか。

　　(A) Glamping enthusiasts （　　　　　　　　　）

　　(B) Avid gamers （　　　　　　　　）

　　(C) Forestry students （　　　　　　　　）

　　(D) Internet service providers （　　　　　　　　　）

3. **What are guests expected to do?** 　ゲストたちは何をすると思われますか。

　　(A) Explore the desert （　　　　　　　　　）

　　(B) Research solar power （　　　　　　　　）

　　(C) Disconnect from the digital domain （　　　　　　　　）

　　(D) Focus on safety （　　　　　　　　）

■ それでは、実際に音声を聞いて設問に答えましょう。 🔊 Audio① 24-28

1. **Where will guests stay?**

    (A) In animal sanctuaries

    (B) On tour buses

    (C) On houseboats

    (D) In tents

2. **Who are the most likely listeners?**

    (A) Glamping enthusiasts

    (B) Avid gamers

    (C) Forestry students

    (D) Internet service providers

3. **What are guests expected to do?**

    (A) Explore the desert

    (B) Research solar power

    (C) Disconnect from the digital domain

    (D) Focus on safety

■ スクリプトの空所を埋めながら、音声の内容を確認しましょう。 ⤶ 🔊 Audio① 25

Questions 1 through 3 refer to the following [1]_____.

W: Panacea is a small and exclusive, signal-free, 100% solar powered luxury [2]_____ _____ _____ that sits on 40 acres in the high desert. It provides an eco-conscious sanctuary where travelers can truly unplug and unwind. In order to [3]_____ in the pace of nature, guests are to completely remove themselves from the outside world by [4]_____ _____ _____ _____ _____ and leaving computers at home or in assigned safes on camp.

■ まずは設問と選択肢の内容を20秒くらいで確認しましょう。その後、音声を聞いて各設問に答えましょう。

1. What kind of company is HPDQ?

   (A) A computer manufacturer

   (B) A business consultancy

   (C) A head-hunting firm

   (D) A travel agency

2. What is the speaker's purpose?

   (A) To hire drivers

   (B) To educate journalists

   (C) To recruit sales staffers

   (D) To promote social media

3. Who is the intended audience?

   (A) Tech-savvy job seekers

   (B) Sports enthusiasts

   (C) High school teachers

   (D) Newsroom producers

■ スクリプトの空所を埋めながら、音声の内容を確認しましょう。   ↻ 🔊 Audio① 30

Questions 1 through 3 refer to the following advertisement.

M: HPDQ is a global industry leader in news and social media intelligence. We [1]_____ _____ to over 32,000 companies around the world to help them [2]_____ _____ and make more informed decisions. We have experienced significant growth in the market since our entry in 2016 and have a need to add to our passionate team. We are looking for [3]_____ _____ _____ _____ _____ in our sales section, whose mission is to educate medium to large businesses on the impact of our insights as we pioneer a [4]_____ _____ _____.

TOEIC® L&RのPart 7では3つの文書を読み設問に応える問題が出題されています。使われている素材はレター、Eメール、メモ、広告などがあります。

シングルパッセージ、ダブルパッセージの場合と同様に、文書の全てを読んでから設問に答えるのではなく、まずは英文のタイトルや冒頭部分に目を通し、主旨を素早く捉えることが重要です。そして、設問文から3つの文書の内のどれを読むことでその問に対する正解を見つけることができるのかを判断することも重要なポイントになります。

■ まずは設問文だけを読んで、問われている内容を確認し、3つのパッセージの内のどれを読む必要があるかを考えてみましょう。

パッセージ（○で囲む）

1. What can reasonably be inferred about Sam Lewis? （1 / 2 / 3）
2. What can reasonably be inferred about Dover Music? （1 / 2 / 3）
3. In the second e-mail, line 1, the word "dire" is closest in meaning to （1 / 2 / 3）
4. What is probably true about Alice? （1 / 2 / 3）
5. Which of the following is NOT true about Dover Music? （1 / 2 / 3）

Questions 1-5 refer to the following advertisement and e-mails.

《Passage 1》

Why Use Dover?

For over 50 years we have offered a premium repair service to musicians all over the UK. Whether it's a youngster needing an emergency fix before an exam or a seasoned professional wanting a customised overhaul, our team can help support your playing.

Here at Dover our ethos is to inspire and support musicians, and our brass repair workshop is on hand for you 6 days a week. We are proud professional members of the National Association of Musical Instrument Repairers and play an active role in the repair community. NAMIR was founded in 1993 to help ensure and promote a high quality of craftmanship within the repair community in the UK.

Here at Dover Music we have 4 highly skilled brass repairers on site. The team are on hand to help with any brass-related repairs from Monday-Saturday 9:00 A.M. - 6:00 P.M.

Our qualified brass repairers can help with servicing and repair work on a host of brass instruments from Soprano Cornet down to Bb Tuba. We can help advise on maintenance and general care, as well as complete 'on-the-spot' repairs and major overhauls.

《Passage 2》

From:	Sam Lewis <slbone@yeehaw.com>
To:	Customer Support <cs@dovermusic.com>
Subject:	urgent repair
Date:	September 17

I'm writing to ask for help repairing the slide on my trombone. This is urgent, as I have a performance this coming Saturday. You reconditioned my horn two years ago, and it has been working fine until this week, but suddenly the slide is sticking and I fear the rails may be bent. May I bring it in for immediate attention? If so, do I need to schedule an appointment?

I look forward to hearing from you at your earliest convenience.

Thank you.

Sam Lewis

《Passage 3》

From:	Alice <Alice@dovermusic.com>
To:	Sam Lewis <slbone@yeehaw.com>
Subject:	Re: urgent repair
Date:	September 18

Dear Mr. Lewis,

Thank you for reaching out to us. We understand your situation is dire, but please understand, so is ours. We can no longer deal with wind instruments without very strict safety precautions, due to the pandemic. For the time being, we accept instruments only through couriers, with no direct visits. In fact, we are already beyond our capacity.
Mr. Dover has asked me to convey his regards. We have been honored to work with a musician of your stature. Under the circumstances, however, and given your tight schedule, there is no way for us to accommodate your request. We hope to be able to help once the situation becomes more settled. Please don't hesitate to contact us going forward.

Sincerely,

Alice

Customer Support

Dover Music

■ 設問文の内容と読むべきパッセージが特定できたら、実際に設問の答えを考えてみましょう。

1. What can reasonably be inferred about Sam Lewis?

   (A) He is a brass band conductor.

   (B) He is an eminent musician.

   (C) He is frequently in touch with Dover Music.

   (D) He is a close friend of Mr. Dover.

2. What can reasonably be inferred about Dover Music?

   (A) It is a small, local company.

   (B) It is an international conglomerate.

   (C) It manufactures brass instruments.

   (D) It has few loyal customers.

3. In the second e-mail, line 1, the word "dire" is closest in meaning to

   (A) dear   (C) severe

   (B) clear   (D) mere

4. What is probably true about Alice?

   (A) She is an amateur trombonist.

   (B) She has known Sam Lewis longer than Mr. Dover.

   (C) She has only recently been hired.

   (D) She acts on Mr. Dover's behalf.

5. Which of the following is NOT true about Dover Music?

   (A) It is closed on Sundays.

   (B) It is active in NAMIR.

   (C) It handles repairs on clarinets.

   (D) It has a small staff.

1 聞き耳トレーニング／Part 1&2

📶 Audio① 34

音声を聞いて聞こえたほうに〇をつけ、正解をチェックした後フレーズの意味を確認しましょう。

1. be (about / around) to begin
2. be (off / of) limits
3. hold a (cup / cap)
4. small but (thriving / surviving)
5. the (counting / accounting) section
6. (schedule / reschedule) it

Part 1 From the following (A) to (D), choose the one statement that best describes what you see in the picture.

📶 Audio① 35-36

1. Ⓐ Ⓑ Ⓒ Ⓓ

2. Ⓐ Ⓑ Ⓒ Ⓓ

Part 2 From the following (A) to (C), choose the best response to the statement you will hear.

📶 Audio① 37-38

1. Mark your answer. Ⓐ Ⓑ Ⓒ

2. Mark your answer. Ⓐ Ⓑ Ⓒ

3. Mark your answer. Ⓐ Ⓑ Ⓒ

フレーズを聞き取り、空所に入る適語を選びましょう。正解をチェックした後、日本語の意味と合わせて確認しましょう。

1. ( ) my office　私のオフィスを模様替えする

2. the ( ) room　待合室

3. keep the ( ) on A　Aに焦点を合わせ続ける

4. ( ) an interior decorator　インテリアデザイナーに相談する

5. ( ) for help　助けを求める

6. a new ( ) of work　新しい仕事

(A) consult　(B) focus　(C) call　(D) line　(E) redecorate　(F) waiting

Part 3　Listen to a conversation and answer the following questions.　📶 Audio① 40-42

Office　　　　　　　　　　　　Waiting Room

Space A

Space C

Space B

Space D

1. What does the man want the woman to do?

　(A) Order a sofa

　(B) Give some advice

　(C) Consult a painter

　(D) Call for help

2. Look at the graphic. Where is the sofa?

　(A) Space A　　　　　(C) Space C

　(B) Space B　　　　　(D) Space D

3. What will the man most likely do next?

　(A) Ask the woman to sit down

　(B) Order some new books

　(C) Focus on a new line of work

　(D) Consult a professional decorator

フレーズを聞き取り、空所に入る適語を選びましょう。正解をチェックした後、日本語の意味と合わせて確認しましょう。

1. achieve (　　) sales　記録的売上を達成する
2. market (　　)　市場占有率
3. (　　) up with A　Aと提携する
4. make a (　　) on A　Aの頭金を支払う
5. sales (　　)　販売部員
6. a (　　) client　見込み客
7. increasing (　　)　配当金の増額

> (A) dividends　(B) tie　(C) share　(D) deposit　(E) representatives
> (F) record　(G) prospective

Part 4　Listen to a talk and answer the following questions.　🔊 Audio① 44-46

1. Who is the speaker addressing?
   (A) A group of sales representatives
   (B) An online marketeer
   (C) A prospective client
   (D) An international investor

2. How can the company's customers best be described?
   (A) Generous
   (B) Wealthy
   (C) Uninformed
   (D) Disinterested

3. What is the company's focus this year?
   (A) Updating the supply chain
   (B) Increasing dividends for stockholders
   (C) Selling more ships
   (D) Avoiding bankruptcy

日本語訳を参考にして、次の英文の間違いを見つけましょう。訂正した箇所の表現をしっかりと覚えましょう。

1. I referred a dictionary for spelling.

   私はスペルを確かめようと辞書を確認した。

2. Josh stayed at the hostel for several day.

   ジョシュはそのホステルに数日泊まった。

3. I haven't been able sleeping for a few days.

   私は2、3日眠れていません。

4. Stay touch.

   連絡を取り合いましょう。

5. My visa has extended by one year.

   私はビザを一年間延長してもらった。

6. Thanks for to come.

   来てくれてありがとう。

7. For more information regard the product, see page 7.

   商品についての詳細は7ページをご覧ください。

8. They used to issue a quarter magazine.

   彼らはかつて3ヶ月毎に雑誌を発行していた。

Part 5

From the following (A) to (D), choose the best answer to complete the sentences below.

1. There are ------- flaws in your proposal.

   (A) several   (B) none   (C) too   (D) every

2. Please stay in touch with ------- by e-mail.

   (A) myself   (B) me   (C) it   (D) itself

3. The deadline for that project has been -------, since the supply chain was interrupted.

   (A) reduced   (B) completed   (C) extended   (D) overcome

4. Information about stock dividends can be found in the ------- report.

   (A) quarter   (B) quartered   (C) quarterly   (D) quarters

5. Please ------- to the memo from the section chief about the new dress code.

   (A) refer   (B) read   (C) study   (D) show

6. This memo is posted for reference purposes for the convenience of those who were unable ------- the meeting

(A) who attend   (B) to attend   (C) attending   (D) attended

7. You will receive an e-mail, at the address you entered in the purchase form, ------- the main conditions of your purchase.

(A) confirming   (B) confirmed   (C) to be confirmed   (D) confirms

8. Office building rents continue to trend downward and the business environment remains ------- .

(A) challenge   (B) to challenge   (C) challenging   (D) challenged

Part 6   From the following (A) to (D), choose the best answer to complete the text below.

Questions 1-4 refer to the following e-mail.

From: Middleoftheroad <devineditor@middleoftheroad.com>
To: fauxbeliever@yeehaw.com

Welcome to *Middle of the Road*

Thanks for ---**1.**--- to our mailing list. We won't spam you, we promise! We'll just send you a monthly newsletter that features some of the previous month's most popular posts and any updates we'd like you to know about, as well as very occasional e-mails ---**2.**--- new issue releases and exclusive offers just for our subscribers.

You can unsubscribe at any time, but we hope you don't, because nothing makes us happier than the ongoing relationships we build with our readers. ---**3.**---.

If you ever have any questions, feel free to e-mail me at devineditor@middleoftheroad.com or respond to this or any future e-mail and I'll get ---**4.**--- to you as soon as I can.

Thanks again.

---

1. (A) subscribe
   (B) subscribed
   (C) subscribing
   (D) subscriber

2. (A) regarding
   (B) replacing
   (C) releasing
   (D) remaining

3. (A) Actually, they can sometimes annoy us.
   (B) In fact, we pride ourselves on them.
   (C) In addition, they will likely purchase more.
   (D) Furthermore, we make use of some of them.

4. (A) ahead
   (B) forward
   (C) behind
   (D) back

健康・医療・環境

音声を聞いて聞こえたほうに〇をつけ、正解をチェックした後フレーズの意味を確認しましょう。

1. (cross / across) a bridge

2. (lead / read) a race

3. (want / wait) my turn

4. feel under the (weather / feather)

5. become (depressed / depressing)

6. get a (hole / hold) of you

Part 1　From the following (A) to (D), choose the one statement that best describes what you see in the picture.　📶 Audio① 48-49

1. Ⓐ Ⓑ Ⓒ Ⓓ　　　　2. Ⓐ Ⓑ Ⓒ Ⓓ

Part 2　From the following (A) to (C), choose the best response to the statement you will hear.　📶 Audio① 50-51

1. Mark your answer.　Ⓐ Ⓑ Ⓒ

2. Mark your answer.　Ⓐ Ⓑ Ⓒ

3. Mark your answer.　Ⓐ Ⓑ Ⓒ

フレーズを聞き取り、空所に入る適語を選びましょう。正解をチェックした後、日本語の意味と合わせて確認しましょう。

1. the ( ) company　保険会社

2. process a ( )　請求の手続きをする

3. send the ( )　申請書を提出する

4. ( ) injury　業務災害

5. a ( ) meeting　組合の会合

6. a company ( )　会社の代表者

(A) claim　(B) representative　(C) forms　(D) insurance　(E) employee　(F) union

Part 3　Listen to a conversation and answer the following questions.　 Audio① 53-55

1. What are the speakers discussing?
   (A) An insurance claim
   (B) A union meeting
   (C) A word-processing problem
   (D) An employee benefits package

2. Who are the speakers expecting a call from?
   (A) An insurance company representative
   (B) An angry employee
   (C) A noted politician
   (D) The police department

3. What possible problem does the woman mention?
   (A) A customer may sue the company.
   (B) The union may object to a company policy.
   (C) Their insurer may reject their claim.
   (D) Forms and documents were mistakenly sent to the wrong party.

フレーズを聞き取り、空所に入る適語を選びましょう。正解をチェックした後、日本語の意味と合わせて確認しましょう。

1. (　　) control technology　騒音防止テクノロジー
2. take (　　) noise　不要な騒音を取り除く
3. (　　) up to 90%　90％まで取り除く
4. a (　　) system　換気装置
5. highly (　　) solutions　非常に効果的な解決策
6. low-(　　) noise　低周波の騒音

(A) eliminate　(B) ventilator　(C) unwanted　(D) effective　(E) frequency　(F) noise

Part 4　Listen to a talk and answer the following questions.　 Audio① 57-59

1. Who is the speaker most likely addressing?
   (A) Private homeowners suffering from noise pollution
   (B) Company representatives interested in a quieter work environment
   (C) Recording studio engineers
   (D) Music school teachers

2. What does the speaker say about this technology?
   (A) It has no rivals.
   (B) It cancels all noises.
   (C) It improves ventilation.
   (D) It has an attractive shape.

3. What does the speaker NOT mention?
   (A) The size of the product
   (B) Sources of noise
   (C) High-frequency sounds
   (D) Economical solutions

日本語訳を参考にして、次の英文の間違いを見つけましょう。訂正した箇所の表現をしっかりと覚えましょう。

1. The only alternate is to take a few days off.
   唯一の選択肢は2、3日休暇をとることだ。

2. Prices in the country are much higher as before.
   その国の物価は以前よりもはるかに高くなっている。

3. The student whom played the leading role in the play was excellent.
   その劇で主役を演じた学生は素晴らしかった。

4. The experience will turn out valuably after you graduate from college.
   大学卒業後にその経験が役に立つでしょう。

5. My sister is staying at my room by the time she finds a new apartment.
   姉は新しいアパートが見つかるまで私の部屋に泊まることになっている。

6. If she had driven a little more carefully, she will have not get involved in the accident.
   彼女がもう少し注意深く運転していれば、事故に巻き込まれずに済んだのに。

Part 5 From the following (A) to (D), choose the best answer to complete the sentences below.

1. People with a high daily intake of vitamin C are three times less likely to have the illness ------- those with unhealthy diets.

   (A) as   (B) yet   (C) than   (D) rather

2. The test kit will be ------- in stopping the spread of influenza at national borders.

   (A) value   (B) valuation   (C) valuably   (D) valuable

3. If the novel virus had been contained much earlier, the company ------- had to dramatically reduce the workforce.

   (A) wouldn't have   (B) won't have   (C) wouldn't   (D) hasn't

4. A recent survey found that people believed the treatment to be an ------- to heart transplants.

   (A) alternative   (B) alternate   (C) altruistic   (D) altar

5. Women ------- experience the therapy face an increased risk of getting breast cancer.

   (A) whom   (B) whose   (C) who   (D) what

6. The rainy season affects the mood of everyone in our department, and it is quite gloomy ------- summer begins.

   (A) but   (B) until   (C) moreover   (D) if

7. In order to ------- down on paper-based waste, employees are encouraged to bring their own coffee cups to work.

    (A) cut   (B) make   (C) put   (D) keep

8. The company health plan initiation fee will ------- be deducted from your first month's salary.

    (A) automation   (B) automated   (C) automatically   (D) automatic

5 速読マスター★素早く重要な情報を見つける／Part 7

次の英文に素早く目を通し、2つの質問に60秒以内で答えましょう。解答は日本語・英語のどちらでも構いません。

As a result of changing weather patterns, due to the increase of the earth's temperature, we can expect much stronger winds this summer. In addition, there should be an increase in rainstorms and the possibility of hurricanes. These severe weather conditions will continue through the warm months and start to fade around the end of September. It can be assumed that this will be a continuous summer pattern unless the earth's temperature starts to decrease.

1. 夏に起こると予期されることは何ですか。3つ答えましょう。

   _____   _____   _____

2. 1.で答えた事柄はいつ終わりを迎えますか。

   _____

Part 7   Read passages and answer the following questions.

Questions 1-5 refer to the following weather report and memo.

> As a result of changing weather patterns, due to the increase of the earth's temperature, we can expect much stronger winds this summer. In addition, there should be an increase in rainstorms and the possibility of hurricanes. These severe weather conditions will continue through the warm months and start to fade around the end of September. It can be assumed that this will be a continuous summer pattern unless the earth's temperature starts to decrease.

To: All employees
From: Departmental Services

Due to weather conditions, we will have to make some structural changes to the building over the next month. This will include replacing windows with shatterproof plastic. We will also be installing some storm shutters that will automatically close during severe storms. While the shutters are closed, you will not be able to open your windows or to look outside. This will be for your own safety. We apologize ahead of time for the construction noise and any inconvenience this may cause. Our sound system will be equipped to receive live radio broadcasts from the state emergency system in the event of a storm, so that you can keep up to date on the weather and its progress.

Sincerely,

Maxwell Short
Director of Departmental Services

1. **What is NOT one result of the increase in the earth's temperature?**
   (A) Longer summers
   (B) Increased hurricanes
   (C) More rainstorms
   (D) More intense winds

2. **When will the weather conditions stop?**
   (A) At the beginning of fall
   (B) The following year
   (C) During the warm months
   (D) In early spring

3. **Why is the company putting in new shutters?**
   (A) Possible hurricanes
   (B) Increased profits
   (C) Milder weather
   (D) Improved views

4. **What time of year will the shutters probably close?**
   (A) January
   (B) June
   (C) October
   (D) During the winter

5. **Why is Mr. Short making an apology?**
   (A) For any future increased noise levels
   (B) For not making the improvements earlier
   (C) For restricting the view of the storms
   (D) For the loud noise of the sound system

1 聞き耳トレーニング／Part 1&2

 Audio① 60

音声を聞いて聞こえたほうに〇をつけ、正解をチェックした後フレーズの意味を確認しましょう。

1. walk through a (field / feed)
2. (road / load) an airplane
3. (rock / lock) some suitcases
4. No, not (yet / that).
5. annual (leaf / leave)
6. go (aboard / abroad)

Part 1 From the following (A) to (D), choose the one statement that best describes what you see in the picture.

Audio① 61-62

1. Ⓐ Ⓑ Ⓒ Ⓓ

2. Ⓐ Ⓑ Ⓒ Ⓓ

Part 2 From the following (A) to (C), choose the best response to the statement you will hear.

Audio① 63-64

1. Mark your answer. Ⓐ Ⓑ Ⓒ
2. Mark your answer. Ⓐ Ⓑ Ⓒ
3. Mark your answer. Ⓐ Ⓑ Ⓒ

フレーズを聞き取り、空所に入る適語を選びましょう。正解をチェックした後、日本語の意味と合わせて確認しましょう。

1. see A (　　) Aを見送る
2. won't (　　) 上手くいかないだろう
3. catch a (　　) タクシーに乗る
4. Thanks for the (　　). コツを教えてくれてありがとう。
5. arrangements for (　　) 出発の手配
6. live (　　) 地元で暮らす

(A) tip　(B) work　(C) departure　(D) cab　(E) off　(F) locally

Part 3　Listen to a conversation and answer the following questions.　 Audio① 66-68

1. **What are the speakers discussing?**
   (A) Arrangements for the man's departure
   (B) The woman's illness
   (C) The man's fear of flying
   (D) The best time to take a trip

2. **What will the man most likely do?**
   (A) Cancel his travel plans
   (B) Tip the taxi driver less
   (C) Take a train to the airport
   (D) See the woman to the hospital

3. **What can we infer about the woman?**
   (A) She works in a restaurant.
   (B) She lives locally.
   (C) She needs an eye test.
   (D) She has just met the man.

3 表現マスター★チャンクで覚える必須用語 2／Part 4　Audio① 69

フレーズを聞き取り、空所に入る適語を選びましょう。正解をチェックした後、日本語の意味と合わせて確認しましょう。

1. a family (　　) business 家族所有経営の事業

2. a wide (　) of A　多種多様なA

3. a tea (　)　喫茶店、カフェ

4. a nature (　)　自然遊歩道

5. (　) sourced products　地元で仕入れられた生産物

6. at a very (　) price　とても手頃な値段で

7. time and (　)　何度も

8. spend some (　) time　充実した時間を過ごす

(A) barn　(B) again　(C) selection　(D) owned and run　(E) reasonable
(F) trail　(G) locally　(H) quality

Part 4　Listen to a talk and answer the following questions.　📶 Audio① 70-72

What You Can Do at Kamas Hill Farm

◆ Strawberry Picking
◆ Afternoon Meals
◆ Hiking
◆ Livestock Management

---

1. How could Kamas Hill Farm best be described?

(A) As a suburban amusement park

(B) As a rural recreation area

(C) As a nature conservancy

(D) As an agricultural cooperative

2. Look at the graphic. According to the speaker, which of the following is most likely NOT on offer now?

(A) Strawberry picking　　　(C) Hiking opportunities

(B) Afternoon meals　　　(D) Livestock management

3. What can the customers do?

(A) Have some luxury cuisine at the restaurant

(B) Refresh themselves by planting some vegetables

(C) Spend time with their family without spending too much

(D) Learn how to manage a business in the countryside

日本語訳を参考にして、次の英文の間違いを見つけましょう。訂正した箇所の表現をしっかりと覚えましょう。

1. The train was delaying by heavy snow.

   列車は豪雪によって遅れた。

2. The country's economy shrunk 15% a year while the 2000s.

   その国の経済は2000年代に年間15％縮小した。

3. It was surprising that the company had bankrupt.

   その会社が倒産したのは驚きであった。

4. The economic situation in the world is expecting to worsen.

   世界の経済状況は悪化すると考えられている。

5. The president of the company became aware for the dangers of smoking.

   その会社の社長は喫煙の危険に気付いた。

6. The city is the best famous for its many old churches and architectures.

   その街は多くの古い教会や建築物で最も有名である。

Part 5 From the following (A) to (D), choose the best answer to complete the sentences below.

1. Her flight was ------- due to turbulence, so Ms. Smith was unable to attend the meeting.

   (A) delayed   (B) relieved   (C) recovered   (D) deteriorated

2. Because of the pandemic, all travel plans are on ------- until further notice.

   (A) call   (B) duty   (C) time   (D) hold

3. Many airlines are likely to ------- bankrupt unless they get government support.

   (A) do   (B) go   (C) break   (D) have

4. Every year airport officials screen millions of items, including some banned items valued to the ------- of $40,000.

   (A) much   (B) cost   (C) expense   (D) amount

5. Travelers need to be ------- of local festivals and other events when attempting to book reservations at area hotels.

   (A) attentive   (B) applicable   (C) aware   (D) contemptuous

6. Summer holiday travel ------- to hit record lows this year due to high gasoline prices.

   (A) expects   (B) is expected   (C) have expected   (D) expecting

7. Meetings of the club may be canceled ------- holiday or vacation periods at the discretion of the board of directors.

   (A) during   (B) still   (C) while   (D) once

8. You can search the international route timetable and check the ------- schedule for your flight on this website.

   (A) lately   (B) later   (C) latest   (D) late

Part 6   From the following (A) to (D), choose the best answer to complete the text below.

Questions 1-4 refer to the following advertisement.

We offer a 10-day tour for an independent-minded traveler with an eye on the budget and keen to experience as much as possible. ---**1.**---. The group size is never more than five guests, and your professional driver-guide provides a ---**2.**--- of information as you travel through an ever-changing landscape. The itinerary takes in the classic wildlife destinations of the northern circuit, beginning with a peaceful night at an Ariba riverside lodge to unwind after what may have been a long journey.

Tanager National Park is first, ---**3.**--- famous for its concentrations of wildlife at the Tanager River during the mid-year dry season and a rewarding destination throughout the year. Home to large numbers of elephants and other heavyweight animals such as buffaloes and giraffes, the wild woods of Tanager compare well with the open plains of the Sanager, where you are on the ---**4.**--- for migrating wildebeest herds and their predators in season. A full-day safari on the flat floor of the Niobe Crater provides more opportunities to spot the Big 5 (lions, leopards, elephants, rhinos and buffaloes) and perhaps flamingos and hippos in the Crater wetlands.

---

1. (A) You will experience more than you can handle.
    (B) This safari has the advantage of more nights than usual on this route.
    (C) Few chances remain to act as land surveyors.
    (D) A safari seldom gets the attention it deserves.

2. (A) wealth   (C) fortune
    (B) cost   (D) bank

3. (A) best   (C) most
    (B) biggest   (D) greatest

4. (A) observation (C) view
    (B) reserve   (D) lookout

1 聞き耳トレーニング／Part 1&2

🔊 Audio① 73

音声を聞いて聞こえたほうに〇をつけ、正解をチェックした後フレーズの意味を確認しましょう。

1. (use / buy) a smartphone
2. taking (note / notes)
3. let (us / me) know
4. (extending / attending) a lecture
5. whole (staff / stuff)

6. (set / bet) up a meeting
7. go (smoothly / smooth)
8. wearing (earphone / earphones)
9. on (tap / top) of the cabinet
10. (what / that) time

Part 1 From the following (A) to (D), choose the one statement that best describes what you see in the picture.

🔊 Audio① 74-75

1. Ⓐ Ⓑ Ⓒ Ⓓ

2. Ⓐ Ⓑ Ⓒ Ⓓ

Part 2 From the following (A) to (C), choose the best response to the statement you will hear.

🔊 Audio① 76-77

1. Mark your answer. Ⓐ Ⓑ Ⓒ

2. Mark your answer. Ⓐ Ⓑ Ⓒ

3. Mark your answer. Ⓐ Ⓑ Ⓒ

フレーズを聞き取り、空所に入る適語を選びましょう。正解をチェックした後、日本語の意味と合わせて確認しましょう。

1. the ( ) in Philadelphia　フィラデルフィアでの会議
2. the ( ) for my presentation　私のプレゼン用のスライド
3. the ( ) in sales　売上げの増加
4. over the ( ) 5 years　過去5年間にわたって
5. each ( )　各部署
6. a percentage of ( ) growth　年間成長率
7. accurately ( )　正確に反映する
8. ( ) for half of our sales　売上げの半分を占める
9. cosmetics ( )　化粧品の売上げ
10. ( ) on presentation software　プレゼン用ソフトの専門家

(A) division　(B) sales　(C) slides　(D) annual　(E) experts
(F) account　(G) last　(H) increase　(I) reflect　(J) conference

Part 3 Listen to a conversation and answer the following questions.　 Audio① 79-81

1. How will the man show the overall sales increase?
   (A) Bar graph
   (B) Line graph
   (C) Pie chart
   (D) Scatter chart

2. What can be said about sales in the cosmetics division?
   (A) Sales have grown rapidly.
   (B) Sales have not decreased.
   (C) Sales are down.
   (D) Sales are picking up slowly.

3. What advice does the woman finally give to the man?
   (A) Go with the pie chart
   (B) Give up the presentation
   (C) Ask someone in marketing
   (D) Check the sales report again

フレーズを聞き取り、空所に入る適語を選びましょう。正解をチェックした後、日本語の意味と合わせて確認しましょう。

1. orientation (　) オリエンテーション冊子
2. check-in (　) 受付
3. at all (　) 常にずっと
4. orientation (　) オリエンテーションプログラム
5. Human (　) Department　人事部
6. employee (　) package　社員福利厚生制度
7. life (　) coverage　生命保険の補償（範囲）
8. (　) plan　年金計画
9. (　) employees　正社員
10. 15-minute (　)　15分休憩

> (A) booklet　(B) Resources　(C) break　(D) insurance　(E) full-time
> (F) times　(G) benefits　(H) program　(I) pension　(J) table

Part 4　Listen to a talk and answer the following questions.　 Audio① 83-85

1. What will be the topic of the first presentation?
   (A) Company rules
   (B) Job descriptions
   (C) Vacation packages
   (D) Employee benefits package

2. How long will the orientation program last?
   (A) Two hours
   (B) Half a day
   (C) One day
   (D) One week

3. What department does Ms. Wendy Hillerman work in?
   (A) The Orientation Department
   (B) The Accounting Department
   (C) The Human Resources Department
   (D) The Sales Department

日本語訳を参考にして、次の英文の間違いを見つけましょう。訂正した箇所の表現をしっかりと覚えましょう。

1. Let's start the meeting at 10:00 sharply.

   会議を10時きっかりに始めましょう。

2. Bob encouraged me joining the workshop.

   ボブは私がその研修会に参加するように励ましてくれた。

3. The document is avail online.

   その書類はオンラインで手に入ります。

4. Which you arrive at the station, please give me a call.

   駅に着いたら、私に電話してください。

5. Our morning meeting is usually bored.

   私たちの朝礼はたいてい退屈なものだ。

6. Let's finish the project for two months.

   2か月でそのプロジェクトを終えましょう。

7. Let's talk about how to present our product to prospect customers.

   我々の製品の見込み客への提供の仕方について話しましょう。

8. Our company's success is due to the quality of it staff.

   わが社の成功はスタッフの質のおかげです。

Part 5 From the following (A) to (D), choose the best answer to complete the sentences below.

1. The meeting will begin at 1:00 -------.

   (A) sharp   (B) before   (C) after   (D) later

2. ------- you arrive at the airport, please call me right away.

   (A) While   (B) When   (C) Which   (D) Where

3. The agenda for the conference is ------- online.

   (A) available   (B) availed   (C) availing   (D) avail

4. In this seminar you will learn a lot about the best ways to present our product to ------- customers.

   (A) lengthy   (B) prospective   (C) ubiquitous   (D) profile

5. The president's so-called motivational speeches are usually -------.

   (A) bored   (B) boring   (C) bore   (D) boredom

6. If it goes according to plan, we should be turning a profit ------- less than six months.

   (A) when   (B) beyond   (C) in   (D) furthermore

7. That company's success is largely due to its innovative marketing strategy, as well as to the quality of ------- personnel.

   (A) its   (B) them   (C) it   (D) their

8. The company encourages employees ------- training seminars to improve productivity and professional development.

   (A) attending   (B) to attend   (C) attended   (D) attend

5 速読マスター★素早く重要な情報を見つける／Part 7

次の英文に素早く目を通し、2つの質問に60秒以内で答えましょう。解答は日本語・英語のどちらでも構いません。

1. 男性の問題は何ですか。

_____

2. 男性はミーティングで何をすることになっていますか。

_____

M: Have you started the meeting? I'm stuck in traffic.

W: Yes, we're just getting underway. When do you think you can get here?

M: I'm not sure. It's a real jam. I guess you'd better tell everyone I can't make it.

W: Well, that won't do. We can't proceed without your presentation.

Part 7   Read a passage and answer the following questions.

Questions 1-5 refer to the following text-message chain.

Jim Alboni [9:01 A.M.]:

Have you started the meeting? I'm stuck in traffic.

Loretta Bale [9:02 A.M.]:

Yes, we're just getting underway. When do you think you can get here?

Jim Alboni [9:03 A.M.]:

I'm not sure. It's a real jam. I guess you'd better tell everyone I can't make it.

Loretta Bale [9:04 A.M.]:

Well, that won't do. We can't proceed without your presentation.

Jim Alboni [9:05 A.M.]:

I can text you a copy of my notes, and you can read them out.

Loretta Bale [9:06 A.M.]:

I think it will be better to postpone this until you can get here.

Richard Traherne [9:07 A.M.]:

Let me jump in here to say that I agree with Loretta.

Jim Alboni [9:08 A.M.]:

Oh, all right, I see I'm outnumbered. I'll get there as soon as I can. I'll keep you posted about my progress.

Loretta Bale [9:09 A.M.]:

OK. In the meantime, I'll try to stall by going over the details of the changes in the blueprints with the clients.

Jim Alboni [9:10 A.M.]:

That's a great idea. Just buy me some time.

Loretta Bale [9:11 A.M.]:

You're on.

1. **What kind of business does Mr. Alboni most likely work for?**
   - (A) Food industry
   - (B) Architectural design
   - (C) Software development
   - (D) Online sales

2. **At 9:10 A.M., what does Mr. Alboni mean when he writes, "Just buy me some time."?**
   - (A) Offer the clients a discount
   - (B) Send me the schedule
   - (C) Slow down the proceedings
   - (D) Increase my salary

3. **What will Ms. Bale most likely do next?**
   - (A) Text Mr. Alboni copies of the blueprints
   - (B) Call Mr. Traherne to explain the situation
   - (C) Search online maps for alternate routes for Mr. Alboni
   - (D) Apologize to the clients for Mr. Alboni's delay

イベント

美術展・パーティなど

1 聞き耳トレーニング／Part 1&2

🔊 Audio① 86

音声を聞いて聞こえたほうに〇をつけ、正解をチェックした後フレーズの意味を確認しましょう。

1. hold (a tray / trays)
2. next to a (statue / stature)
3. (sow / show) up at a party
4. a (goodluck / potluck) party
5. (can / can't) make it
6. (sit / sick) in bed

Part 1　From the following (A) to (D), choose the one statement that best describes what you see in the picture.

🔊 Audio① 87-88

1. Ⓐ Ⓑ Ⓒ Ⓓ　　　　　　2. Ⓐ Ⓑ Ⓒ Ⓓ

Part 2　From the following (A) to (C), choose the best response to the statement you will hear.

🔊 Audio① 89-90

1. Mark your answer.　Ⓐ　Ⓑ　Ⓒ
2. Mark your answer.　Ⓐ　Ⓑ　Ⓒ
3. Mark your answer.　Ⓐ　Ⓑ　Ⓒ

フレーズを聞き取り、空所に入る適語を選びましょう。正解をチェックした後、日本語の意味と合わせて確認しましょう。

1. foot the (　) 　勘定を支払う
2. get A's (　) up 　Aに期待を持たせる
3. (　) A out 　Aを数に入れない
4. (　) the party 　パーティを調整する
5. be (　) with the responsibility 　責任がある
6. if that's the (　) 　それが本当であれば
7. make a (　) 　提案する
8. go (　) 　さあ、どうぞ

(A) coordinate　(B) bill　(C) stuck　(D) count　(E) case　(F) hopes
(G) ahead　(H) suggestion

Part 3　Listen to a conversation and answer the following questions.　📶 Audio① 92-94

1. Where is the party likely to be held?

(A) At a pizza restaurant

(B) At a French restaurant

(C) At the office

(D) At the president's house

2. Who will pay the bill for the party?

(A) All the staff members

(B) Some volunteer members

(C) Employees at Sal's Pizza

(D) The company president

3. What will the man most likely do next?

(A) Ask for a suggestion

(B) Call Sal's Pizza

(C) Coordinate the party

(D) Make a proposal for the party

フレーズを聞き取り、空所に入る適語を選びましょう。正解をチェックした後、日本語の意味と合わせて確認しましょう。

1. by ( )　予約して
2. without adult ( )　大人の監督なしで
3. bronze ( )　銅の鋳物工場
4. ( ) shoe　爪先の空いた靴
5. wheelchair ( )　車椅子で利用できる
6. ( ) glasses　安全メガネ

(A) foundry　(B) accessible　(C) appointment　(D) safety　(E) open-toed
(F) supervision

Part 4　Listen to a talk and answer the following questions.　Audio① 96-98

1. What is the main business of Art Castings?
   (A) Producing metal sculptures
   (B) Guiding tour groups
   (C) Instructing future actors
   (D) Promoting museum safety

2. What can be inferred about the foundry?
   (A) It was established recently.
   (B) It is potentially dangerous.
   (C) It can accommodate overnight guests.
   (D) It is a non-profit organization.

3. Look at the graphic. How much should a senior with two children under 10 pay for the tour?
   (A) Nothing　　　　　　(C) $5.00
   (B) $4.00　　　　　　 (D) $9.00

日本語訳を参考にして、次の英文の間違いを見つけましょう。訂正した箇所の表現をしっかりと覚えましょう。

1. Why aren't you give her another chance?

   彼女にもう一度チャンスを与えてはどうですか。

2. I have met some people whose survived the war.

   その戦争を生き延びた人にあったことがあります。

3. Cancer can be cured if it finds early.

   ガンは早期に発見されると治療可能だ。

4. You should do what you normal do.

   いつもやっていることをするべきですよ。

5. The store offering a great variety of imported foods.

   その店は様々な輸入食品を取り揃えている。

6. Today's discussion is focusing our new smoking policy.

   本日の議論は新しい喫煙方針に焦点を当てます。

Part 5 From the following (A) to (D), choose the best answer to complete the sentences below.

1. Corporate ------- of sporting events is a mainstay of our operations.

   (A) investment   (B) payment   (C) saving   (D) sponsorship

2. Why ------- you chip in to the office pool for his retirement party?

   (A) haven't   (B) aren't   (C) don't   (D) weren't

3. Employees delivered meals to the elderly ------- have trouble getting out of the house.

   (A) whom   (B) which   (C) whose   (D) who

4. Show the bus ticket stub and get a 15% discount ------- the lift ride and admission fee to the Art Museum.

   (A) for   (B) as   (C) like   (D) by

5. Another fascinating day trip ------- at the Agriculture Museum, a reconstruction of life in a thatched homestead 250 years ago.

   (A) to find   (B) is found   (C) has found   (D) is finding

6. The children were delighted to be in a soccer stadium that is ------- used by professional soccer players.

   (A) normal   (B) norms   (C) normally   (D) norm

7. Our working art gallery ------- a unique venue for small events.

    (A) offerings   (B) offers   (C) offering   (D) offer

8. The National Museum in the city ------- the world's largest collection of Chinese artifacts, artwork, and imperial archives.

    (A) holds   (B) affects   (C) admits   (D) responds

Part 6   From the following (A) to (D), choose the best answer to complete the text below.

Questions 1-4 refer to the following advertisement.

> Join our professional wildlife guides for a 3- to 5-hour whale watching tour, starting in the picturesque fishing village of historic Stetson and traveling through the spectacular San Marco Islands. Our extensive whale-spotting network has ---**1.**--- us a 90% sighting success rate. Our whale watching tour focuses ---**2.**--- magnificent orcas (killer whales) and majestic humpback whales, plus other marine wildlife such as porpoises, sea lions, seals and bald eagles.
>
> Our vessels are expedition-style Zodiacs, specifically designed for marine mammal viewing. ---**3.**---. This increases passenger comfort and safety, as well as ---**4.**--- the chance of seasickness. Our Explorer II (open) and Express (semi-covered) vessels use water jets, which are extremely safe for marine mammals. All three of our ocean-going vessels are equipped with washrooms.

1. (A) made
   (B) taken
   (C) given
   (D) had

2. (A) at   (C) in
   (B) on   (D) of

3. (A) They travel over the top of the water instead of pounding through it.
   (B) They take on water rather than floating on it.
   (C) They alternately consume and expel water.
   (D) They prefer fresh water to salt water.

4. (A) increasing
   (B) leveling
   (C) boarding
   (D) reducing

1 聞き耳トレーニング／Part 1&2 🔊 Audio② 01

音声を聞いて聞こえたほうに○をつけ、正解をチェックした後フレーズの意味を確認しましょう。

1. buy a (sweet / suit)
2. wait (on / in) line
3. (quite / quiet) warm
4. take a (while / whale)
5. stop (on / by) the shop
6. (take / bake) a cake

Part 1 From the following (A) to (D), choose the one statement that best describes what you see in the picture. 🔊 Audio② 02-03

1. Ⓐ Ⓑ Ⓒ Ⓓ

2. Ⓐ Ⓑ Ⓒ Ⓓ

Part 2 From the following (A) to (C), choose the best response to the statement you will hear. 🔊 Audio② 04-05

1. Mark your answer. Ⓐ Ⓑ Ⓒ
2. Mark your answer. Ⓐ Ⓑ Ⓒ
3. Mark your answer. Ⓐ Ⓑ Ⓒ

フレーズを聞き取り、空所に入る適語を選びましょう。正解をチェックした後、日本語の意味と合わせて確認しましょう。

1. a (　) houseplant　耐寒性の観葉植物
2. have a good (　) of A　Aを豊富に取り揃えている
3. (　) up A's apartment　Aのアパートを明るくする
4. Here you (　).　はい、どうぞ。
5. Now you're (　).　それはいいですね。
6. This will (　) nicely.　これで十分でしょう。
7. You're in (　).　ついてますね。
8. It's on (　).　セール中です。

> (A) luck　(B) hardy　(C) go　(D) brighten　(E) talking　(F) do
> (G) selection　(H) sale

Part 3　Listen to a conversation and answer the following questions.　📶 Audio② 07-09

1. Where are the speakers?
   - (A) At a real estate agency
   - (B) At a building site
   - (C) At a nursery
   - (D) At a language school

2. What does Alex want to do?
   - (A) Paint his apartment
   - (B) Buy a plant
   - (C) Find a new place
   - (D) Study harder

3. What does the man mean when he says, "Now you're talking."?
   - (A) He likes the woman's voice.
   - (B) He is not a native English speaker.
   - (C) He enjoys small talk.
   - (D) He finds the store's suggestion appropriate.

フレーズを聞き取り、空所に入る適語を選びましょう。正解をチェックした後、日本語の意味と合わせて確認しましょう。

1. new (　)　新しくマイホームを手にした人
2. a large (　) of money　多額のお金
3. (　) your home　家に家具を備え付ける
4. (　) wood　再生利用された木材
5. (　) pipes　鋼鉄製のパイプ
6. light (　)　電球

> (A) bulbs　(B) reclaimed　(C) steel　(D) homeowners　(E) equip　(F) sum

Part 4　Listen to a talk and answer the following questions.　🔊 Audio② 11-13

1. **Who does the speaker represent?**
   (A) An industrial design firm
   (B) A DIY shop
   (C) A real estate company
   (D) An interior decorator

2. **What kinds of designs are being introduced?**
   (A) Lighting fixtures
   (B) Home floorplans
   (C) Industrial layouts
   (D) Store decors

3. **Who is the speaker most likely addressing?**
   (A) Industrial equipment engineers
   (B) Construction company laborers
   (C) Home loan guarantors
   (D) Budget-conscious shoppers

4 文法・語法マスター★語感覚を身につける／Part 5

日本語訳を参考にして、次の英文の間違いを見つけましょう。訂正した箇所の表現をしっかりと覚えましょう。

1. I haven't spoken to him for late.

   最近彼と話していません。

2. The new smartphone can be fully charge in half an hour.

   新しいスマートフォンは30分でフル充電可能です。

3. He has two sons, also he is a grandfather of two girls.

   彼には二人の息子がいて、二人の女の子の祖父でもある。

4. The virus affects people of all ages between young babies to the elderly.

   そのウィルスは幼い赤ん坊から高齢者まであらゆる年齢の人々に影響を与えている。

5. The shopping mall is with walking distance of the station.

   ショッピングモールは駅から徒歩圏内にあります。

Part 5 From the following (A) to (D), choose the best answer to complete the sentences below.

1. Department stores have been struggling of -------.

   (A) past   (B) late   (C) early   (D) timely

2. The new electric motorbike can be ------- at home the same way you charge your cellular phone.

   (A) charged   (B) to charge   (C) charging   (D) charge

3. Food is purchased every day, ------- price is a key factor for grocery shoppers.

   (A) and so   (B) also   (C) but   (D) when

4. The city's factory outlets ------- shoppers a great way to find real bargains on name-brand items.

   (A) offering   (B) to offer   (C) will be offered   (D) offer

5. ------- bespoke tailors to discount shops, we have something for every taste and budget.

   (A) From   (B) Along   (C) Of   (D) In

6. Bottled water is common and ------- in all local grocery shops and supermarkets.

   (A) availabilities   (B) available   (C) avail   (D) availability

7. We have two big supermarkets with late night services, one department store and even a sports gym all ------- a 5-minute walk.

   (A) within   (B) when   (C) where   (D) while

8. Better World credit cards ------- at major supermarket and department store chains and many tourist destinations.

   (A) has been accepting   (B) accepting   (C) are accepted   (D) accepts

5 速読マスター★素早く重要な情報を見つける／Part 7

次の英文に素早く目を通し、2つの質問に60秒以内で答えましょう。解答は日本語・英語のどちらでも構いません。

What sets Elpah apart is our careful planning and a creative process that always involves you, our customers.

We don't simply let you pick a few characteristic elements like color or wood type just to call our service customizable. Neither do we assemble mass-produced furniture parts by hand just to validate calling our products handmade. Elpah puts heart into the made-to-order furniture business.

1. Elpah社は何を販売する会社ですか。

   _____

2. Elpah社が打ち込んでいることは何ですか。

   _____

Part 7   Read passages and answer the following questions.

Questions 1-5 refer to the following advertisement and e-mails.

Elpah Furniture

What sets Elpah apart is our careful planning and a creative process that always involves you, our customers.

We don't simply let you pick a few characteristic elements like color or wood type just to call our service customizable. Neither do we assemble mass-produced furniture parts by hand just to validate calling our products handmade. Elpah puts heart into the made-to-order furniture business.

Our process begins with a visit from our clients. We will present 142 unique furniture styles for you to draw inspiration from and for us to use as a foundation for building your furniture. What follows is the application of practical elements into an otherwise creative collaboration. — [1] —. We'll ask questions regarding product specifications, such as "How wide is your dining room and how large would you prefer your dining table to be?" and "Your choice of bed frame is tasteful, but will it fit in your bedroom?" Count on us to consider the nuances of the room or space that you want us to furnish.

We offer you six different wood species to choose from: walnut, oak, maple, hickory, cherry, and alder. — [2] —.

Your choice of wood and finish can transform the look of your furniture. If this is your first time making these major decisions for custom furniture, don't worry; we will gladly help you choose combinations that will achieve the look and feel you desire.

Furniture that is artistic and shows our hard work — these are the elements that speak to any devoted homemaker. The knowledge that a lot of hard work and skill went into creating a piece of furniture creates a high level of sentiment. — [3] —. Also, these types of furniture promise quality and stylistic timelessness. These are the ones that stay in the family for years, even generations, to come.

At Elpah Furniture, we take pride in our ability to produce the highest quality wooden furniture that suits the style, preferences, and living space of each client. — [4] —.

Contact us to schedule a showroom visit.

□□□

From:	kittyg@kmail.com
To:	hello@elpahfurniture.com
Subject:	custom sofa
Date:	July 24

Hello,

I am interested in a custom-made sofa. According to your website, it seems you require a showroom visit to begin the ordering process. Is that correct? I do not live in the area, and I am wondering if we can do this all by e-mail? Also, I notice that your showroom is only open Tues.-Fri. from 10:00 A.M. to 5:00 P.M. Doesn't that limit potential customers who can only visit on weekends?
I look forward to hearing from you about these matters.

Kate Grover

From: hello@elpahfurniture.com

To: kittyg@kmail.com

Subject: custom sofa

Date: July 26

Dear Ms. Grover,

Thank you for your interest in our line of custom-made furniture. Unfortunately, we do not make sofas. Our products are all handcrafted from wood. So if you are interested in a cabinet, console, sideboard, or table for your living room, we will do our utmost to meet your needs.

Our showroom hours reflect the fact that we spend our own weekends devoted to completing the pieces our customers have ordered. We are a family business, and most of our work is time-consuming and painstaking.

We wish you all the best in your search for a sofa.

Sincerely,

Nate Elpah

1. In which of the positions marked [1], [2], [3], and [4] does the following sentence best belong?

   "Furthermore, we provide several beautiful options for finishes so that you can make your furnishing your own."

   (A) [1]

   (B) [2]

   (C) [3]

   (D) [4]

2. What is indicated in the advertisement about Elpah Furniture?

   (A) They sometimes use mass-produced parts.

   (B) They visit each customer's house if necessary.

   (C) They ask clients about the size of their rooms.

   (D) They only provide service to regular clients.

3. In the advertisement, the phrase "speak to" in paragraph 6, line 1, is closest in meaning to

   (A) are meaningful for
   (B) communicate with
   (C) translate as
   (D) are fundamental to

4. Which of the following can reasonably be inferred about Kate Grover?

   (A) She has a very large home.
   (B) She is a furniture wholesaler.
   (C) She has not examined the catalogue.
   (D) She is a website designer.

5. Which of the following can reasonably be inferred about Nate Elpah?

   (A) He does not like using e-mail.
   (B) He has previously done business with Kate Grover.
   (C) He works only on weekends.
   (D) He is a woodworker.

Unit 10 不動産・広告・経済など

1 聞き耳トレーニング／Part 1&2

Audio② 14

音声を聞いて聞こえたほうに〇をつけ、正解をチェックした後フレーズの意味を確認しましょう。

1. Some cars are (packed / parked).
2. (hold / fold) a handle
3. (could / couldn't) agree
4. on the (19th / 90th) Street
5. used to (living / live) alone

Part 1

From the following (A) to (D), choose the one statement that best describes what you see in the picture.

Audio② 15-16

1. Ⓐ Ⓑ Ⓒ Ⓓ

2. Ⓐ Ⓑ Ⓒ Ⓓ

Part 2

From the following (A) to (C), choose the best response to the statement you will hear.

Audio② 17-18

1. Mark your answer.　Ⓐ　Ⓑ　Ⓒ
2. Mark your answer.　Ⓐ　Ⓑ　Ⓒ
3. Mark your answer.　Ⓐ　Ⓑ　Ⓒ

フレーズを聞き取り、空所に入る適語を選びましょう。正解をチェックした後、日本語の意味と合わせて確認しましょう。

1. doublecheck the (　　)　設計図を再確認する
2. something (　　)　何か不適切なこと
3. be in the (　　) place　場所がおかしい
4. two inches (　　)　2インチずれている
5. such a big (　　)　そのような大ごと
6. be worth (　　)　やり直すに値する

(A) wrong　(B) off　(C) amiss　(D) redoing　(E) blueprints　(F) deal

Part 3　Listen to a conversation and answer the following questions.　 Audio② 20-22

1. **What are the speakers discussing?**
   (A) A blue painting
   (B) A possible construction error
   (C) A new contract
   (D) A building location

2. **What did the man do?**
   (A) He went back two times.
   (B) He signed a deal.
   (C) He built a wall.
   (D) He took a measurement.

3. **What does the woman imply?**
   (A) Money is the primary consideration.
   (B) The man needs to find a better deal.
   (C) The man is wrong.
   (D) It's easy to make changes.

フレーズを聞き取り、空所に入る適語を選びましょう。正解をチェックした後、日本語の意味と合わせて確認しましょう。

1. simple yet fully modern (　)　シンプルだが全く現代的な住宅
2. (　) logs　最高品質の丸太
3. (　) every need　あらゆる要望に応える
4. the flexibility to (　)　注文通りに作る柔軟さ
5. Our pricing is (　).　私たちの価格は他社よりも安いです。
6. our (　) staff　我々の経験豊富なスタッフ
7. your dreams are (　)　あなたの夢が実現される

> (A) competitive　(B) residences　(C) fulfilled　(D) meet　(E) customize
> (F) experienced　(G) top-quality

Part 4　Listen to a talk and answer the following questions.　Audio② 24-26

1. What is the purpose of this prospectus?
   (A) To sell wooden houses
   (B) To promote a design team
   (C) To analyze dreams
   (D) To compete in hiring staff members

2. What does the speaker mean when she says, "the flexibility to customize"?
   (A) There will be no extra taxes.
   (B) The designs can be altered.
   (C) The buildings have no blueprints.
   (D) The work can be done at various times.

3. Who will most likely be interested in this?
   (A) Those seeking an apartment to rent
   (B) Those investing in commercial properties
   (C) Those planning to live in a rural area
   (D) Those designing skyscrapers

日本語訳を参考にして、次の英文の間違いを見つけましょう。訂正した箇所の表現をしっかりと覚えましょう。

1. The news of the sudden merger set his nerves at edge.
   突然の合併の知らせに彼は神経を尖らせた。

2. The new smartphone is likely hit the market by the next month.
   新しいスマートフォンが来月までに市場に出る見込みだ。

3. Our customers tend preferring more compact products.
   我が社の顧客はより小型の製品を好む傾向がある。

4. Effective measures have not taken by the government to beat depression.
   不況を打破する効果的な措置が政府によって取られていない。

5. The bank decided to cut interesting rates in response to worsening economy.
   その銀行は悪化する経済状態に対応して利率を下落させることに決めた。

Part 5 From the following (A) to (D), choose the best answer to complete the sentences below.

1. The sudden downturn in the stock market has set everyone ------- edge.
   (A) on   (B) by   (C) at   (D) in

2. This recession has forced us to revise all our profit -------.
   (A) products   (B) projections   (C) properties   (D) proponents

3. That advertising campaign ------- beyond all expectations.
   (A) success   (B) successful   (C) succeeded   (D) succeeding

4. According to our latest projections, profits are ------- to stay flat in the next quarter.
   (A) likely   (B) possible   (C) tend   (D) favorite

5. Economists ------- to disagree about the root causes of the recession.
   (A) trend   (B) lend   (C) send   (D) tend

6. If no countermeasures ------- taken, the region's economy will spiral down.
   (A) had been   (B) had   (C) are   (D) were

7. If ------- rates stay where they are, the boom will continue.
   (A) interested   (B) interesting   (C) interest   (D) to interest

8. A lot of people went bankrupt ------- real estate values plummeted.
   (A) although   (B) because   (C) even though   (D) as if

次の英文に素早く目を通し、2つの質問に60秒以内で答えましょう。解答は日本語・英語のどちらでも構いません。

1. Scrod International Suppliersは何種類の配達方法を提供していますか。

   _____

2. Scrod International Suppliersに連絡をすると何が手に入りますか。

   _____

Part 7 Read a passage and answer the following questions.

Questions 1-3 refer to the following advertisement.

Scrod International Suppliers
Specializing in providing items from foreign countries

- Clothing
- Food
- Electronics
- Jewelry
- Automobiles

- Magazines
- Newspapers
- Dinnerware
- Art
- Commercial equipment

Offering different forms of delivery services

*Express mail   *Sea Freight   *Air Freight   *Next-day delivery

Allow us to take care of all your transportation needs!

Contact us to receive a full-color catalog of all the products that we have available

Newport Hill
1732 Kingsford Highway
Boomtown, NY 12968
(432) 555-8463

Monday-Friday 8:00 A.M.- 6:00 P.M.
Also visit our website at www.scrodis.com

---

1. **What type of product is NOT being offered by Scrod International Suppliers?**

   (A) Jewels
   (B) Sea Freight
   (C) Dishes
   (D) Cars

2. **What does this company offer customers?**

   (A) Only one form of delivery
   (B) Free jewelry
   (C) Printing services
   (D) International products

3. **Where is this company located?**

   (A) Scrod
   (B) New York
   (C) Outside of the U.S.
   (D) All over the world

1 聞き耳トレーニング／Part 1&2

🔊 Audio② 27

音声を聞いて聞こえたほうに○をつけ、正解をチェックした後フレーズの意味を確認しましょう。

1. (sit / set) some tables
2. hang (on / up) the phone
3. stay (on / at) my desk
4. care for (second / seconds)
5. eat (out / here) for lunch

Part 1

From the following (A) to (D), choose the one statement that best describes what you see in the picture.

🔊 Audio② 28-29

1. Ⓐ Ⓑ Ⓒ Ⓓ

2. Ⓐ Ⓑ Ⓒ Ⓓ

Part 2

From the following (A) to (C), choose the best response to the statement you will hear.

🔊 Audio② 30-31

1. Mark your answer. Ⓐ Ⓑ Ⓒ
2. Mark your answer. Ⓐ Ⓑ Ⓒ
3. Mark your answer. Ⓐ Ⓑ Ⓒ

フレーズを聞き取り、空所に入る適語を選びましょう。正解をチェックした後、日本語の意味と合わせて確認しましょう。

1. go out for a ( ) to eat　軽く食べに行く
2. make ( ) plans　はっきりと予定を決める
3. a 15-minute ( ) from our office　オフィスから歩いて15分
4. in ( ) of the office　オフィスの前で
5. That ( ) good.　それは良さそうだね。
6. ( ) out　満員になる、大混雑する
7. get ( ) out　雨天中止になる
8. ( ) our plan　予定を最終決定する

(A) front　(B) bite　(C) pack　(D) rained　(E) definite　(F) finalize
(G) walk　(H) sounds

Part 3　Listen to a conversation and answer the following questions.　🔊 Audio② 33-35

1. What are the speakers discussing?
   (A) Plans to go out
   (B) Business meetings
   (C) Sport events
   (D) Travel plans

2. What can be assumed about the Thai restaurant?
   (A) It is very spicy.
   (B) It is far from the office.
   (C) It is popular.
   (D) It is very expensive.

3. Which of the following would allow the man to meet the woman earlier?
   (A) If he takes a day off
   (B) If he skips his softball game
   (C) If it rains on Friday
   (D) If the restaurant extends its hours

フレーズを聞き取り、空所に入る適語を選びましょう。正解をチェックした後、日本語の意味と合わせて確認しましょう。

1. a (　　) company　フランチャイズ店を持つ会社

2. (　　) learning experience　対話型の学習経験

3. the (　　) arts　料理（という芸術）

4. (　　) creativity　創造性を刺激する

5. a (　　) environment　居心地の良さそうな環境

6. in (　　) kitchens　子どもが使いやすいキッチンで

7. (　　) franchise support　継続的なフランチャイズサポート

(A) interactive　(B) ignite　(C) culinary　(D) kid-friendly　(E) welcoming
(F) franchise　(G) ongoing

Part 4　Listen to a talk and answer the following questions.　Audio② 37-39

1. Who is the speaker most likely addressing?

(A) Celebrity chef promoters

(B) Kindergarten teachers

(C) Young children

(D) Potential franchise owners

2. What does the speaker mean when she says, "a life-long love of the culinary arts"?

(A) Children will develop a lasting interest in cooking.

(B) Teachers will offer art appreciation courses.

(C) YCU will open a museum.

(D) Franchises will focus on long-term business models.

3. What does the speaker say about the kitchens?

(A) They are environmentally friendly.

(B) They are easy for children to use.

(C) They are made by the speaker.

(D) They are designed by amicable teachers.

日本語訳を参考にして、次の英文の間違いを見つけましょう。訂正した箇所の表現をしっかりと覚えましょう。

1. The politician was admitted to the locally hospital.

   その政治家は地元の病院に入院した。

2. Service charges are including in the room rate.

   サービス料は宿泊料金に含まれています。

3. Her husband is sociable, still Maggie is very shy.

   夫は社交的ですが、マギーはとても内気です。

4. Ours tomatoes are one hundred percent organic.

   私たちのトマトは完全な有機栽培です。

5. I usually make airplane appointments over the web.

   私はいつもウェブで飛行機の予約をします。

Part 5　From the following (A) to (D), choose the best answer to complete the sentences below.

1. ------- more menu innovation, many fast food restaurant chains will lose future business.

   (A) Throughout　　(B) According to　　(C) Without　　(D) Due to

2. Meet with new classmates and friends in a ------- pub for a fun social evening.

   (A) locals　　(B) locality　　(C) local　　(D) locally

3. Situated at the end of the restaurant, the room ------- up to 20 diners and offers the perfect setting for special occasions.

   (A) seats　　(B) excepts　　(C) gains　　(D) plans

4. A service charge of 15% ------- in restaurant bills in Paris.

   (A) is included　　(B) includes　　(C) has included　　(D) to include

5. Many restaurants in the area, including Top-Notch Burgers, ------- to provide catering for parties.

   (A) has started　　(B) to start　　(C) have started　　(D) starting

6. Coco Café serves ------- cuisine a la carte or at a buffet for breakfast, lunch and dinner.

   (A) international　　(B) prompt　　(C) attentive　　(D) eventual

7. Our weekday lunch menu features 4 or 6 courses, ------- our dinner and weekend lunch menu offers 6 or 8 courses.

(A) instead   (B) while   (C) still   (D) between

8. On Saturdays, ------- fantastic dinner features everything from soup to noodles and curries and is accompanied by live jazz.

(A) us   (B) we   (C) ours   (D) our

Part 6 From the following (A) to (D), choose the best answer to complete the text below.

Questions 1-4 refer to the following advertisement.

Q features a menu that highlights fresh local foods. The cost of the tasting menu is 298 dollars per person.

When making your ---**1.**---, please indicate any dietary restrictions. Due to the complexity of the menu, it may not be possible to ---**2.**--- all restrictions and food allergies.

All reservations are confirmed by phone at least three days prior. Any cancellations must be made at least 48 hours prior to the time of the reservation to avoid a 298 dollar (plus tax) per person late cancellation charge. If we are unable to ---**3.**--- with you, your reservation will be canceled one day prior to the reservation at 5:00 P.M. ---**4.**---.

1. (A) party
   (B) menu
   (C) reservation
   (D) dishes

2. (A) regard
   (B) accommodate
   (C) understand
   (D) register

3. (A) call
   (B) discuss
   (C) meet
   (D) confirm

4. (A) We thank you for your understanding.
   (B) It is delicious.
   (C) You are welcome.
   (D) See you next time.

1 聞き耳トレーニング／Part 1&2

📶 Audio② 40

音声を聞いて聞こえたほうに○をつけ、正解をチェックした後フレーズの意味を確認しましょう。

1. (live / leave) a meeting

2. shake (a hand / hands)

3. free of (change / charge)

4. the salary (range / raise)

5. there (won't be / want to be) any

Part 1　From the following (A) to (D), choose the one statement that best describes what you see in the picture.

📶 Audio② 41-42

1. Ⓐ Ⓑ Ⓒ Ⓓ   2. Ⓐ Ⓑ Ⓒ Ⓓ

Part 2　From the following (A) to (C), choose the best response to the statement you will hear.

📶 Audio② 43-44

1. Mark your answer.　Ⓐ　Ⓑ　Ⓒ

2. Mark your answer.　Ⓐ　Ⓑ　Ⓒ

3. Mark your answer.　Ⓐ　Ⓑ　Ⓒ

フレーズを聞き取り、空所に入る適語を選びましょう。正解をチェックした後、日本語の意味と合わせて確認しましょう。

1. your performance (　) 業績評価
2. my sales (　) 売り上げノルマ
3. give A a (　) Aを昇給する
4. a (　) approach 静観的な取り組み方
5. That makes (　). それは筋が通っている。
6. be in a (　) spot ひどく困っている
7. get a (　) bonus 高額のボーナスをもらう
8. put A (　) college Aを大学に合格させる、通わせる

> (A) review　(B) hefty　(C) sense　(D) quota　(E) wait-and-see
> (F) tight　(G) raise　(H) through

Part 3　Listen to a conversation and answer the following questions.　📶 Audio② 46-48

1. What kind of position does the woman most likely hold?
   (A) Performance artist
   (B) Company president
   (C) Sales representative
   (D) College teacher

2. What did the woman receive?
   (A) An increase in salary
   (B) A managerial commendation
   (C) A new position
   (D) A college degree

3. How can the woman's final comment best be described?
   (A) Relieved
   (B) Cynical
   (C) Overjoyed
   (D) Satisfied

フレーズを聞き取り、空所に入る適語を選びましょう。正解をチェックした後、日本語の意味と合わせて確認しましょう。

1. our ( ) session　（従業員を）やる気にさせる集会

2. ( ) oneself on A　Aに誇りを持つ

3. ( ) with A　Aと交流する

4. ( ) badge　色分けされたバッジ

5. the winning ( )　勝利チーム

6. develop effective ( )　効果的な戦術を考えつく

7. ( ) against one another　お互いに競い合う

> (A) pride　(B) compete　(C) color-coded　(D) interact　(E) squad
> (F) motivational　(G) strategies

Part 4　Listen to a talk and answer the following questions.　🔊 Audio② 50-52

1. **What is the purpose of this speech?**
   - (A) To introduce a new lighting system
   - (B) To prepare employees for some contests
   - (C) To recruit new staff members
   - (D) To open a corporate athletic center

2. **How can the audience best be described?**
   - (A) It consists of everyone in the company.
   - (B) It is limited to those studying colored lights.
   - (C) It comprises champions from various regions.
   - (D) It includes teams from other companies.

3. **What will most likely happen next?**
   - (A) Employees will receive new job assignments.
   - (B) Color-coded prizes will be distributed.
   - (C) Managers will be assigned secondary roles.
   - (D) Teams will engage in athletic events.

日本語訳を参考にして、次の英文の間違いを見つけましょう。訂正した箇所の表現をしっかりと覚えましょう。

1. You can count on him. He is a safety driver.

   彼はあてにできるよ。運転が安全だからね。

2. Almost people in the section graduated from the best universities.

   その部門のほとんどの人は一流大学を卒業している。

3. The company will force to dismiss nearly half of the employees.

   その会社は従業員の半数近くを解雇せざるを得なくなるだろう。

4. She grew from a young girl into a success businessperson.

   彼女は幼い少女からビジネスパーソンとして出世するまでになった。

5. We're planning to deliver a farewell speech to the graduation.

   卒業生に向けてお別れの挨拶をすることを計画している。

6. If you wish leaving a message, please speak clearly after the tone.

   メッセージを残したい場合は、発信音の後にはっきりと話してください。

7. Please stay here while I pay for us seats.

   座席の代金を支払う間ここにいてください。

Part 5　From the following (A) to (D), choose the best answer to complete the sentences below.

1. Because he is such a ------- long-haul driver, he received a commendation and a bonus.

   (A) safety　　　(B) safe　　　(C) safely　　　(D) safest

2. The number of applicants for that position ------- all expectations.

   (A) scheduled　　　(B) added　　　(C) exceeded　　　(D) surprised

3. To prepare for a job interview, you should ------- questions about your goals as well as your achievements.

   (A) anticipate　　　(B) provide　　　(C) realize　　　(D) deflect

4. Human Resources is responsible for ------- with legal requirements for employee rights.

   (A) compliance　　　(B) survey　　　(C) contact　　　(D) research

5. ------- people in that section have degrees in electrical engineering.

   (A) Almost　　　(B) Most　　　(C) Every　　　(D) Each

6. If the projections are correct, our division will ------- to lay off about a tenth of the staff.

   (A) be forced   (B) have forced   (C) have been forcing   (D) force

7. After we complete the screening process, ------- candidates will be contacted by either phone or e-mail.

   (A) success   (B) succeed   (C) successful   (D) successfully

8. Hanover Pharmaceuticals is currently hiring recent ------- with a strong grounding in the field of biochemistry.

   (A) graduation   (B) graduating   (C) graduated   (D) graduates

Part 6 From the following (A) to (D), choose the best answer to complete the text below.

Questions 1-4 refer to the following letter.

James Devereaux

Managing Director

Devereaux Design

124 Montpelier Road

Greenwood, CO 45312

Dear Mr. Devereaux,

---**1.**---. I would like to invite you to attend our upcoming design department job networking event, which will be held May 30, beginning at 1:00 P.M. We ---**2.**--- to provide our graduating seniors with opportunities to meet business leaders in the area who may be looking for new hires who hold degrees in design.

The event will be held in the Dancy Student Center here at Converse State and will last about two to three hours. If you are ---**3.**--- in attending or sending a company representative to meet with ---**4.**--- students, please let me know at your earliest convenience, so I can reserve a table for you.

Regards,

Nancy Kelly

Head of the Design Department

---

1. (A) It has been far too long since I was last in touch.

  (B) You must have forgotten me by now.

  (C) I am sure you can't make it, but I'm trying anyway.

  (D) This is your last chance.

2. (A) must

  (B) will

  (C) trend

  (D) wish

3. (A) interested

  (B) interesting

  (C) interest

  (D) to interest

4. (A) your

  (B) our

  (C) us

  (D) we

エンターテインメント

1 聞き耳トレーニング／Part 1&2 🔊 Audio② 53

音声を聞いて聞こえたほうに〇をつけ、正解をチェックした後フレーズの意味を確認しましょう。

1. play (a / the) saxophone
2. set (down / on) a bottle
3. I'm afraid (not / it).
4. appreciate the (performance / performing) arts
5. more than (13 / 30) minutes

Part 1 From the following (A) to (D), choose the one statement that best describes what you see in the picture. 🔊 Audio② 54-55

1. Ⓐ Ⓑ Ⓒ Ⓓ   2. Ⓐ Ⓑ Ⓒ Ⓓ

Part 2 From the following (A) to (C), choose the best response to the statement you will hear. 🔊 Audio② 56-57

1. Mark your answer. Ⓐ Ⓑ Ⓒ
2. Mark your answer. Ⓐ Ⓑ Ⓒ
3. Mark your answer. Ⓐ Ⓑ Ⓒ

フレーズを聞き取り、空所に入る適語を選びましょう。正解をチェックした後、日本語の意味と合わせて確認しましょう。

1. three ( ) seats ます席を3つ
2. The ( ) is full. 満席です。
3. a ( ) room 立ち見席
4. by ( ) up 列に並ぶことで
5. first come, first ( ) 早い者勝ち
6. something to ( ) on おやつに食べるもの

(A) snack (B) house (C) lining (D) served (E) box (F) standing

Part 3 Listen to a conversation and answer the following questions.   Audio② 59-61

Schedule	
10:00 A.M.	Ticket Booth Open
1:00 P.M.	First Show
4:00 P.M.	Second Show

1. What should the woman bring with her tomorrow?

   (A) Something to sit on
   (B) Some food
   (C) Something to shelter her from the sun
   (D) Her tickets

2. What can be assumed about the show?

   (A) It is very undesirable.
   (B) It is held outside.
   (C) It is very popular.
   (D) It does not have box seats.

3. Look at the graphic. What time is the woman most likely to arrive tomorrow morning?

   (A) 9:30 A.M.   (C) 1:00 P.M.
   (B) 10:00 A.M.   (D) 4:00 P.M.

フレーズを聞き取り、空所に入る適語を選びましょう。正解をチェックした後、日本語の意味と合わせて確認しましょう。

1. (　　) concerts　身内（私的な）のコンサート
2. theater (　　)　演劇
3. family (　　)　家族の集まり
4. excellent (　　)　素晴らしい音響効果
5. (　　) seating arrangements　用途の広い席の配置
6. the esteemed (　　) firm　尊敬を集める建築事務所
7. a (　　) catering service　一流の出前サービス

(A) architectural　(B) intimate　(C) versatile　(D) reunions　(E) acoustics
(F) top-notch　(G) productions

Part 4　Listen to a talk and answer the following questions.　🔊 Audio② 63-65

1. What is the speaker's purpose?
   (A) To introduce a designer
   (B) To sell property
   (C) To promote a venue
   (D) To arrange for a meeting

2. Which of the following features is mentioned?
   (A) An abundant capacity
   (B) A large stage
   (C) A wooden design
   (D) An absence of competition

3. Which of the following conveniences is mentioned?
   (A) A food service
   (B) A large parking area
   (C) A course in design
   (D) A pet-care facility

日本語訳を参考にして、次の英文の間違いを見つけましょう。訂正した箇所の表現をしっかりと覚えましょう。

1. I'm very exciting that my childhood dream has come true.

   子供の頃からの夢が実現してとても興奮しています。

2. Bear in mind what the weather in London is very changeable.

   ロンドンの天気はとても変わりやすいということを覚えておいてください。

3. One of her jobs at the hospital is to assist patients with them meals.

   病院での彼女の仕事の一つは患者の食事を手伝うことだ。

4. Playing the piano is his own way to express him.

   ピアノを弾くことが彼の自己表現の方法である。

5. It took three days to transportation the goods by air freight.

   商品を航空便で輸送するのに3日かかった。

6. Another options to get to the civic center is to take a cab.

   市民センターまで行くもう一つの選択肢はタクシーに乗ることです。

Part 5 From the following (A) to (D), choose the best answer to complete the sentences below.

1. The record company has ------- that they are preparing to make the band's catalogue available on the internet.

   (A) confronted   (B) comforted   (C) confirmed   (D) conflicted

2. The amusement park is building the world's first Ferris wheel ------- transparent heart-shaped gondolas.

   (A) having   (B) to have   (C) had   (D) has

3. The tour of the toy factory made the little boy very -------.

   (A) to excite   (B) excited   (C) exciting   (D) excites

4. We would like to announce ------- our new evening show will start this Friday at 11 P.M.

   (A) it   (B) what   (C) that   (D) however

5. The hall hosts many classical music concerts, and the members of the audience often express ------- profound enjoyment of the music.

   (A) their   (B) they   (C) theirs   (D) themselves

6. Create your own personal 3D theater experience and surround ------- in the latest Blu-ray movies.

(A) your   (B) yourself   (C) yours   (D) you

7. ------- the concert you can enjoy a wonderful 5-course dinner which you can choose from our special menu.

(A) Before   (B) Around   (C) Beneath   (D) Like

8. Below the amusement park, a moving walkway ------- visitors through the Underwater Cove Aquarium.

(A) transports   (B) transportation   (C) be transported   (D) transporters

Part 6 From the following (A) to (D), choose the best answer to complete the text below.

Questions 1-4 refer to the following information.

There are several ways to visit the museum. For example, it is possible to buy a ticket to the Offoli Gallery at a reserved time, ---1.--- in this way the endless waiting time at the ticket offices. It is also possible to visit the museum by participating in a guided tour of the Offoli Gallery with a fixed schedule. In addition to the visit to the museum, it is also possible to book a ---2.--- tour that includes the Offoli Gallery with a walking tour of the city, or a tour that includes the Academic Gallery. Another ---3.--- is a private visit to the Offoli Gallery, which allows you to visit the museum with an exclusive guide. With a private guide, you can choose the route you prefer. ---4.---. For those who want to take an unusual tour, we suggest visiting the Offoli Gallery, the Barbera Museum and the Picanto Gardens, or you can even follow an itinerary that traces the history of the whole area.

1. (A) participating   (C) revealing
   (B) canceling   (D) avoiding

2. (A) guide   (C) guiding
   (B) guided   (D) to guide

3. (A) option   (C) claim
   (B) requirement   (D) duty

4. (A) Therefore, we expect you to do as you please.
   (B) As a result, we conclude that most tours are too time consuming.
   (C) For example, we propose a combined visit to the Offoli Gallery and the historic center of Ortagio.
   (D) In order to offer this option, we plan to hire guides.

1 聞き耳トレーニング／Part 1&2

📶 Audio② 66

音声を聞いて聞こえたほうに○をつけ、正解をチェックした後フレーズの意味を確認しましょう。

1. take (a place / place)
2. stacked (in / on) bundles
3. pass (through / throughout) a turnstile
4. go by (the train / train)
5. (locate / relocate) the head office
6. pay (with / by) check

Part 1 From the following (A) to (D), choose the one statement that best describes what you see in the picture.

📶 Audio② 67-68

1. Ⓐ Ⓑ Ⓒ Ⓓ

2. Ⓐ Ⓑ Ⓒ Ⓓ

Part 2 From the following (A) to (C), choose the best response to the statement you will hear.

📶 Audio② 69-70

1. Mark your answer. Ⓐ Ⓑ Ⓒ
2. Mark your answer. Ⓐ Ⓑ Ⓒ
3. Mark your answer. Ⓐ Ⓑ Ⓒ

フレーズを聞き取り、空所に入る適語を選びましょう。正解をチェックした後、日本語の意味と合わせて確認しましょう。

1. the air conditioning (　　)　エアコンの温度設定
2. (　　) the dress code　ドレスコードを和らげる
3. get (　　)　拒否される
4. keep up (　　)　身だしなみをきちんとする
5. our (　　) of work　私たちの職種
6. from time to (　　)　時々
7. take A up with the (　　)　Aについて組合に持ちかける

(A) setting　(B) appearances　(C) nixed　(D) time　(E) loosen　(F) union　(G) line

Part 3　Listen to a conversation and answer the following questions.　 Audio② 72-74

1. Where do the speakers most likely work?
   (A) In an air conditioning factory
   (B) In a dress-making shop
   (C) At an amusement park
   (D) At a public relations firm

2. What does the woman suggest about the dress code?
   (A) It's worth discussing with the labor union.
   (B) The man should take off his jacket.
   (C) The man should be satisfied with "casual Fridays."
   (D) It depends on the air conditioning.

3. How can the management's policies best be described?
   (A) Flexible
   (B) Conservative
   (C) Informal
   (D) Lax

フレーズを聞き取り、空所に入る適語を選びましょう。正解をチェックした後、日本語の意味と合わせて確認しましょう。

1. (　　) carriers　ゴミの運搬業者
2. a single (　　)　1つの容器
3. the (　　) of A　Aの良い点
4. the (　　) of A　Aの悪い点
5. the entire (　　)　積み荷全体
6. disposed of in a (　　)　埋立地に処分される
7. current recycling (　　)　現在のリサイクル業務
8. oily (　　)　油のついた段ボール

> (A) cons　(B) load　(C) pros　(D) practices　(E) waste　(F) cardboard
> (G) landfill　(H) container

Part 4　Listen to a talk and answer the following questions.　 Audio② 76-78

1. **What is the speaker's target audience?**
   (A) Water purification scientists
   (B) Industrial polluters
   (C) Garbage truck drivers
   (D) Convenience-seeking citizens

2. **What can be inferred about landfills?**
   (A) They are ecologically beneficial.
   (B) They are handled by specialists.
   (C) They are unfortunate necessities.
   (D) They are vital for developers.

3. **What can be inferred about potential customers?**
   (A) They are willing to pay for this service.
   (B) They are teams of specialists.
   (C) They are managers of landfills.
   (D) They are experts on contamination.

日本語訳を参考にして、次の英文の間違いを見つけましょう。訂正した箇所の表現をしっかりと覚えましょう。

1. All personnel in the company have to be competent in both English or German.

   その会社の全職員は英語とドイツ語の両方に堪能である必要がある。

2. The big raise negotiation was reopened on 2018.

   大規模な賃上げ交渉は2018年に再開された。

3. She didn't attend the meeting because her father's illness.

   父の病気が原因で彼女は会議に出席しなかった。

4. Great numbers of Japanese banks failed since 1992.

   1992年以来多くの数の日本の銀行が倒産している。

5. The company has decided laying off one-third of their employees because of recession.

   不況が原因でその会社は従業員の3分の1を解雇することに決めている。

Part 5 From the following (A) to (D), choose the best answer to complete the sentences below.

1. Our products are ------- durable and light.

   (A) either   (B) yet   (C) both   (D) neither

2. The battery pack needs to undergo -------.

   (A) perspective   (B) passage   (C) intention   (D) inspection

3. The prospectus for that start-up leaves a lot to be -------.

   (A) desired   (B) erased   (C) caused   (D) made

4. The company was founded ------- 1981 and has become a leader in robotics.

   (A) on   (B) at   (C) in   (D) of

5. When the customs clearance process is -------, the package will be delivered promptly.

   (A) complete   (B) starting   (C) underway   (D) initiated

6. They are losing market share ------- of unimaginative and poorly designed products.

   (A) due   (B) because   (C) account   (D) in spite

7. Since 2017 MIS Media ------- a solid reputation as a provider of professional internet services to hundreds of companies worldwide.

    (A) was built   (B) has built   (C) had been built (D) built

8. The company decided ------- some head office functions on September 13, 2019.

    (A) relocating   (B) relocation   (C) relocates   (D) to relocate

5 速読マスター★素早く重要な情報を見つける／Part 7

次の英文に素早く目を通し、2つの質問に60秒以内で答えましょう。解答は日本語・英語のどちらでも構いません。

Dear Mr. Smith:

It has come to our attention that you have refused to pay your bill for our services. According to the contract that you signed with us at the beginning of the year, failure or refusal to pay for services rendered will result in a penalty charge of 10% of the amount due for each month after the billing date. As it has been three months since we last submitted our bill, you have accumulated a penalty of 30%. To stop additional penalty charges from occurring, we strongly suggest that you pay the total amount due by the end of this month.

1. スミス氏が抱えている問題は何ですか。

2. Eメールの送信者はどのような提案をしていますか。

Part 7   Read passages and answer the following questions.

Questions 1-5 refer to the following letter and bill.

Lame O. Services
545 Willard Street
Madison, Wisconsin 53700

March 15, 2020

Mr. Smith

123 International Lane

Boston, Massachusetts 01234

Dear Mr. Smith:

It has come to our attention that you have refused to pay your bill for our services. According to the contract that you signed with us at the beginning of the year, failure or refusal to pay for services rendered will result in a penalty charge of 10% of the amount due for each month after the billing date. As it has been three months since we last submitted our bill, you have accumlated a penalty of 30%. To stop additional penalty charges from occurring, we strongly suggest that you pay the total amount due by the end of this month.

Sincerely,

Bill Johnson

Lame O. Services

Billing Date: December 15, 2019
Account number: 18973-0083
Account name: Smith, William G. 009

Item(s)	Cost per unit	No. of units	Total
Wheel-8457	$54.00	4	$216.00
Tire Rim-00871	$45.00	4	$180.00
Front Cover-072	$4.00	1	$4.00
Dash Display-0120	$50.00	1	$50.00
Car Emblem-09	$20.00	5	$100.00
TOTAL BILL			$550.00

1. **What has Mr. Smith failed to do?**

   (A) Contact Lame O. Services

   (B) Pay on time

   (C) Refuse services

   (D) Make an order

2. **What does Mr. Smith currently owe?**

   (A) $165.00

   (B) $550.00

   (C) $715.00

   (D) 30%

3. **If Mr. Smith makes a complete payment, what will happen?**

   (A) They will not charge him 30%.

   (B) He will stop getting penalty charges.

   (C) He will only owe Lame O. Services $550.00.

   (D) He may make additional purchases.

4. **What does Lame O. Services probably sell?**

   (A) Food products

   (B) Automobile parts

   (C) Paintings

   (D) Computers

5. **What is the most expensive single item?**

   (A) A wheel

   (B) A tire rim

   (C) A front cover

   (D) An emblem

総合演習

Part 1

From the following (A) to (D), choose the one statement that best describes what you see in the picture.

🔊 Audio② 79-80

1. Ⓐ Ⓑ Ⓒ Ⓓ

2. Ⓐ Ⓑ Ⓒ Ⓓ

Part 2

From the following (A) to (C), choose the best response to the statement you will hear.

🔊 Audio② 81-82

1. Mark your answer. Ⓐ Ⓑ Ⓒ

2. Mark your answer. Ⓐ Ⓑ Ⓒ

3. Mark your answer. Ⓐ Ⓑ Ⓒ

Part 3

Listen to a conversation and answer the following questions.

🔊 Audio② 83-85

1. **Where do the speakers most likely work?**

    (A) In a research and development lab

    (B) At a university

    (C) In a hardware store

    (D) At a sporting goods shop

2. **What do the speakers have in common?**

    (A) An interest in geography

    (B) A friendship with referees

    (C) A background in economics

    (D) An aversion to mathematics

3. What will most likely happen next?

(A) The man will revise his ideas.

(B) The man will send his essay to another journal.

(C) The woman will go back to college.

(D) The woman will read the man's article.

Part 4 Listen to a talk and answer the following questions. 🔊 Audio② 86-88

1. Who is most likely to take interest in the service being promoted?

(A) Someone enrolling in a drama school

(B) Someone facing a job transfer

(C) Someone selling antique furniture

(D) Someone training for boxing

3. What can be inferred about the business partnership mentioned?

(A) Ace handles short-distance moves.

(B) Whitfield is an insurance company.

(C) Ace is a securities company.

(D) Whitfield handles box manufacturing.

3. What service is NOT emphasized in this statement?

(A) Friendly advice

(B) Interstate relocation

(C) Customer contentment

(D) Long-term storage

Part 5 From the following (A) to (D), choose the best answer to complete the sentences below.

1. Our research into the trust fund ------- problems that left us with many misgivings.

(A) showing   (B) showed   (C) shown   (D) show

2. Our research and development budget has been cut ------- in half.

(A) almost   (B) together   (C) considerably   (D) drastically

3. The media ------- likely to play up the scandal behind the bankruptcy.

(A) will   (B) are   (C) have   (D) has

4. It would be too ------- to convert all our equipment to the metric system.

(A) high   (B) highly   (C) cost   (D) costly

5. Equity market trend ------- is a field that involves an incredible number of factors.

(A) analysis   (B) analyses   (C) analyze   (D) analytic

 Part 6   From the following (A) to (D), choose the best answer to complete the text below.

Questions 1-4 refer to the following information.

Air cargo is used by global importers and exporters when they need to get goods somewhere rapidly and reliably. While 90% of everything is shipped by ocean freight, air freight connects the world faster, ---**1**.--- China-US shipping time, for example, from 20-30 days by ocean to only three days by air. ---**2**.---. Express air freight is typically handled by one company for the entire shipment lifecycle, going from door to door in under five days. These express air freight shipments are usually smaller (less than one cubic meter and 200 kilograms) than air freight. In a typical season, international air freight rates can range from approximately $2.50-$5.00 per kilogram, ---**3**.--- on the type of cargo you're shipping and available space. International air freight shipments can be significantly larger and may move across multiple carriers during shipment. ---**4**.---, the largest cargo plane, the Atlas 114, can hold an entire train.

1. (A) replacing
   (B) cutting
   (C) organizing
   (D) budgeting

2. (A) International air freight is exactly the same as express freight shipments.
   (B) International air freight has replaced express freight shipments.
   (C) International air freight is the opposite of express freight shipments.
   (D) International air freight and express freight shipments are not the same.

3. (A) depending
   (B) counting
   (C) relying
   (D) calling

4. (A) On the other hand
   (B) No matter what
   (C) As a matter of fact
   (D) In the same way

Part 7 Read a passage and answer the following questions.

Questions 1-2 refer to the following web page.

(PRESCHOOL STORYTIME)

Tuesday, October 27: 10:00 A.M. - 10:30 A.M.

Virtual Event (BiblioGraf)

AGE GROUP: PRESCHOOLERS

EVENT TYPE: VIRTUAL EVENT, STORYTIMES, BOOKS & READING

Enjoy Storytime, on YOUR time! Preschool Storytimes are presented by Children's Librarians from The City Library. New Stories are added weekly and are available for a limited time.

Venue details

Use this link to join the Preschool Storytime session.

(BOOK BABY)

Tuesday, October 27: 11:00 A.M. - 11:30 A.M.

Virtual Event (BiblioGraf)

AGE GROUP: BABIES & TODDLERS

EVENT TYPE: STORYTIMES, BOOKS & READING

Enjoy Book Baby, on YOUR time! These virtual Book Baby sessions are presented by Children's Librarians from The City Library. New Stories are added weekly.

Venue details

Use this link to join the Book Baby session.

(HELLO MUSIC DRUMMING CLASS)

Tuesday, October 27: 3:00 P.M. - 3:30 P.M.

Virtual Event (BiblioGraf)

AGE GROUP: KIDS

EVENT TYPE: MUSIC

Your City Library and Hello Music have come together to provide a special series of virtual drumming classes for children ages 7 and up. Don't miss out — these videos will only be online until Nov 8.

Venue details

Use this link to join the Hello Music Drumming Class.

SWEET READS BOOK CLUB

Tuesday, October 27: 7:00 P.M. - 8:30 P.M.

Virtual Event (ZipZap)

AGE GROUP: SENIORS ADULTS

EVENT TYPE: VIRTUAL EVENT, CONVERSATIONS, BOOKS & READING, BOOK CLUBS

A monthly book club for the Avenues! Discover new books and get to know the faces in your neighborhood. Light refreshments will be provided at each event.

Venue details

Use this link to join the Book Club session.

1. **What do these events have in common?**

   (A) They are all aimed at children.

   (B) They are all focused on storytelling.

   (C) They are all online.

   (D) They are all held at the library.

2. **What can be inferred about Storytime?**

   (A) It involves children listening.

   (B) It is focused on infants.

   (C) It is focused on librarians.

   (D) It involves librarians listening.

▼写真出典
Unit 8, Part 1-2: © Anton_Ivanov / Shutterstock.com
Unit 9, Part 1-2: ©www.hollandfoto.net / Shutterstock.com
Unit 15, Part 1-1: ©sarawuth wannasathit / Shutterstock.com

PRACTICAL EXERCISES FOR THE TOEIC® L&R TEST
実践のためのTOEIC® L&R総合対策問題集

2021年4月5日　初版第1刷発行

著　　者　　川端淳司／Jeffrey Herrick／鈴木順一

発 行 者　　森　信久
発 行 所　　**株式会社　松 柏 社**
　　　　　　〒102-0072　東京都千代田区飯田橋1-6-1
　　　　　　TEL　03 (3230) 4813（代表）
　　　　　　FAX　03 (3230) 4857
　　　　　　http://www.shohakusha.com
　　　　　　e-mail: info@shohakusha.com

装　　幀　　小島トシノブ（NONdesign）
本文レイアウト・組版　松永亮太（有限会社ケークルーデザインワークス）
印　　刷　　日経印刷株式会社
ISBN978-4-88198-770-4
略号＝770

Copyright © 2021 by Junji Kawabata, Jeffrey Herrick and Junichi Suzuki